Even Tougher than Herding Cats

Advice for your management journey

Ger Mulcahy

Copyright Information

First Edition, 2019.

Visit the author's website at
https://www.amusingmulcahy.com

© 2019 Ger Mulcahy. All Rights Reserved.

Table of Contents

Copyright Information 2
Introduction – Who is this book for? 7
    About the title 7
    Why did I write this? 8
    Structure 10
    A big thank you 11
Know 12
    Know Your Role 13
        People Management 14
    Know your stakeholders 18
    Know your values 19
    Know your thinking style 22
    Know your objectives 24
    Know when to start something 27
    Know how to delegate 29
        The Seagull manager 30
        The Monkey Management problem 30
    Know your numbers 32
    Know your strengths 34
    Know your limits 38

Know your organisation 40
Know your industry 43
Know how to manage conflict 45
Know what you don't know 47
Manage 49
    Manage your time 50
        Time planning 52
    Manage your energy 54
    Manage your focus 55
    Manage your health 59
        Physical Health 60
        Sleep 61
        Mental Health 63
    Manage your people 65
    Manage your communications 69
        Email 70
        Instant messaging or Chat 72
        Verbal communication 74
    Manage your reactions 77
    Manage your hiring 82
    Manage your career 85
Be 89
    Be curious 90

Be available 92
Be emotionally intelligent 94
Be vulnerable 96
Be a networker 99
Be politically aware 102
Be honest 104
Be authentic 105
Be organised 107
Be a team player 111
Be a customer advocate 114
Be considerate of others' time 116
Be a continuous learner 118
Be kind 119
Be reasonably unreasonable 121
Be resilient 123
Be consistent 126
Be action-oriented 128
Be accountable 131
Be a role model 133
Be mindful 135
Become 138
Become a storyteller 139
Become a cheerleader 140

Become a critical thinker	142
Become aware of your biases	145
Become a culture carrier	148
Become a D&I champion	152
Become a mentor	154
Become a volunteer	158
Become a (good) leader	160
Conclusion	164
Acknowledgements	167
Bibliography	168
Links Reference	169

Introduction – Who is this book for?

Managing people and organisations can be very challenging. There are plenty of ways to fail, sometimes subtly, which can have long term impact for the people you are responsible for, and sometimes your career. Becoming an accomplished manager is a constant learning exercise, and requires intentional approaches to the everyday challenges we face in management roles.

I'm aiming this book primarily at the proto-managers, at team leaders and junior managers, and those making the transition from junior to mid-level management. It may also benefit those with more experience – after all, we all have blind spots.

In so many organisations, dependable technical, operational, production and creative people get promoted, often with little to zero preparation or support. This book is intended to help provide some hard-learned information to managers who are starting their journey or making transitions to new roles.

About the title

There is a saying in the software development world that managing software engineers is like trying to herd cats. Both groups are independently-minded, may not take direction well and will typically ignore attempts to bond. The phrase is pretty well known - EDS commissioned an advertising campaign showing cowboys herding cats, which is worth a look (if you want to see real cowboys riding herd on CGI cats).

I don't think managing people *is* like herding cats – but to become a good people manager can sometimes feel like it's more difficult! We need to acknowledge the differences between the people and circumstances we manage, and the unique approaches that may be required to get to the best outcomes.

Why did I write this?

I've been managing people for the past 20+ years. I've acted as mentor, coach, cheerleader and often amateur psychologist (note, I am not a doctor, nor do I play one on the Internet).

During that time, I've learned a few things, some of them painfully. Ben Franklin has been quoted as saying *"The things that hurt, instruct."* The most painful lessons are often the ones that stick with us, but it is also sometimes easier to learn from others' mistakes. (To throw in another near-obligatory quote, Elizabeth Roosevelt's advice is to *"Learn from the mistakes of others. You can't live long enough to make them all yourself."*)

I decided to write this book because I feel that there is a gap in information for new, developing and sometimes, experienced managers. If I can help in some way to accelerate the development of people into better managers, then I will consider this to have been worth the time and effort involved in writing it.

I will provide references to other books and materials that I would have loved to encounter as an emerging leader, as well as suggesting focus areas for developing managers to consider.

If you find obvious errors, or things that you strongly disagree with, or references that you think might help in developing an understanding of some of these topics, please feel free to contact me at herdingcats@amusingmulcahy.com. I won't promise that everyone will get a personal response, but I will try to address and incorporate the feedback that I receive.

Structure

This book is **deliberately** short. I've tried to avoid a lot of filler and to focus on providing advice. After all, I believe that's why you're reading the book. It introduces a lot of topics without going into great detail - if you're curious about them, I'm hopeful that you will dig into those subjects in more depth.

I've divided this book up into four sections - *Know, Manage, Be and Become.*

Know covers topics that can be nuanced, but starts with what I would argue is the most important – understanding what your role is.

Manage looks at key areas of focus for anyone, manager or otherwise, and is more about managing oneself than others.

Be is about the behaviours that are helpful to cultivate. It is the most extensive section of the book, primarily because I'm very much focussed on "now" a lot of the time.

Become discusses the approaches that help managers become leaders at all levels in the organisation.

A big thank you

I've dedicated this book to my wife, Katrina, and my three girls, Lia, Lauren and Lily, who often taught me things about managing myself that I wasn't expecting. I love you all - thank you for gifting me the time to write this.

Thank you also to the people who read my blog posts and gave me the encouragement to write more by providing feedback, and to those special people who took the time to help me with proof-reading this book.

Know

Why start with "knowing"? There are pre-requisites that any good or aspiring-to-be-good manager should have or strive to acquire as quickly as possible. Basic knowledge about yourself, your staff, your job and your stakeholders is the fundamental starting point for any management journey. It's also the case that what you know changes as you learn and develop; not just new knowledge replacing the old, but old mental positions becoming invalidated by additional perspective and experience. When I meet with new mentoring groups, I often say "the more I learn, the less I know." I'm not projecting fake humility by saying this. I've reached a point in my life where I realise that I will never have enough time in what remains of my life to learn about everything in which I'm interested. This realisation can result in a sense of mild panic, from time to time. I'll touch on continuous learning in a later section in the book, but one characteristic of learning anything is that it exposes you to new fields of knowledge, of which you will initially be woefully ignorant. Plan on learning those things you need to know as early as possible so that you can start adding value quickly in your new role.

Know Your Role

This requirement may seem tremendously obvious, but new managers are often transitioning from an individual contributor or team lead roles. The rules of operation are often very different in the manager's new position. He or she may have been used to being instructed, or in better organisations may have been given a portfolio of work to execute, as a more junior staff member.

Managers and leaders (and we'll talk about the differences in later parts of the book) are expected to set the direction for their area (and beyond). They are expected to know who their stakeholders are and to know what constitutes success for their manager and the organisation to which they belong.

Additionally, there is an expectation to demonstrate different behaviours to those exhibited by more junior members of staff.

In Ram Charan's book "The Leadership Pipeline" he discusses the changes in behaviour and skills required as individuals make the transition through a development pipeline in an organisation. Some skills are essential to carry through from position to position, and other skills and behaviours are no longer valuable and must be left behind.

To know your role, you should have a clear set of expectations established when you assume responsibility for the position. Agree and document with your manager what the expectations are, and revisit them at least once a year, either as part of or separate from semi-annual performance reviews.

Key to understanding how you're delivering is to understand who you're providing services for. It is also vital to know what your role is not – and who can help fill in gaps when you need help.

One key component for any management or leadership role is, of course, people management, which we'll discuss at a very high level in the next section.

People Management

There are many different styles of people management, just as there are many kinds of people. The approaches we take as managers need to have some level of tailoring to the individual because it is one size does not fit all.

I recently interviewed someone for a team lead role, and he described his approach to people management as "high trust". He went on to say that he likes to give people autonomy wherever possible.

I'm essentially cut from the same mould. I believe we should give people as much autonomy as they can safely handle. The level of freedom will vary from individual to individual, based on experience, expertise and a demonstrated capability to deliver.

Autonomy doesn't mean that people should act entirely independently of you or other team members. It means that they should have sufficient authority to get their work done efficiently without having to check back with their team lead or manager continuously.

In "Turn the Ship Around!", David Marquet describes this approach in action. This book is an easy-to-read story of how, as a submarine captain and then commander, he turned around one of the worst-performing nuclear submarines in the fleet to make it one of the best.

He did this by delegating authority as far down in the ship as made sense. If someone wanted to get his approval to do something, instead of asking for permission, he asked them to phrase it as an intent:

"Sir, I intend to take the ship ahead two-thirds."

The use of intentional language places ownership for the action with the person notifying the submarine captain. It makes them accountable for the task being undertaken and builds confidence in their capabilities on both sides. Once Marquet established this practice, he stopped giving direct orders, which was highly unusual for any military command.

This approach had several benefits. 1) The crew stopped relying on the captain for answers for everything (see the Monkey Management section in the section "Know how to delegate" as the opposite of this. 2) The crew also came to rely on their own technical competence.

The way Marquet subsequently described one of his fundamental tenets was to "Move the authority to where the information is." In other words, ensure that appropriate levels of delegation (something I discuss later) are taking place so that people are empowered to do the job we pay them to do.

Additionally, we can take a "Trust, but Verify" approach. This phrase came to public prominence during the US/Russia nuclear disarmament talks in the 1980s when it was used by Ronald Reagan (although it is based on a Russian proverb). In the case of managing people, to me it means taking a critical view of very high-stakes decisions; this can erode trust if used for every interaction, so it is essential to know when verification is crucial. After all, we are the responsible parties in the event of an issue, so we must perform due diligence for critical or high-stakes activities.

When it comes to reinforcing the desired behaviour, appropriately rewarding and recognising people is vital. Reward and recognition aren't just about their compensation package, although that is a crucial part of any employer-employee contract – after all, most of us work to put a roof over our heads and to feed our families. When someone in your team does something well, it is essential to praise that person in public. Praising in this way sends a clear signal to the organisation as to what "good looks like". Praise should be delivered as soon after the individual displays the desired behaviour as is practical – at a team meeting or a town hall, or with a note to them copying their manager (or yours, depending on the circumstances).

When it comes to correction of unwelcome behaviours, my preference is to do this in private, whether it involves staff, peers or my senior management. I've worked with, and for, managers who publicly castigated staff, and I found it to be both profoundly uncomfortable and unhelpful. If managers "shoot the messenger" they are unlikely to hear bad news in a timely fashion. In fact, by behaving in this way, we are likely to create cultures where burying bad news altogether is the norm. We've probably all worked in organisations where all reports are always "Green" because no-one wants to discuss the unpleasant reality of a missed deadline for fear of getting blasted. This cultural aspect is both unhealthy and unrealistic, in my opinion.

In other words, I adhere to the "praise in public, correct in private" mindset. This approach may not work for you, but during my career, I've found it the best method to motivate people and help them with behavioural challenges. We'll discuss other aspects of people management in the section below "Manage your people".

Know your stakeholders

Success or failure in any management role depends on knowing who your stakeholders are, knowing what is important to them, and understanding how to deliver for them. At the early stages of our careers, stakeholder maps can be pretty simple – the most common stakeholders are your team lead or manager, your peers (yes, you do have a responsibility to them) and the consumers of your output – internal or external client groups.

As our careers develop, our stakeholder groups become increasingly complex, particularly in large organisations. At the more senior levels in a large, regulated enterprise, stakeholders will include internal and external control partners (e.g. Compliance, Legal, Risk, Audit and Regulators), customers, and senior management regionally and globally. This variation can represent a very challenging set of stakeholders to manage effectively, so there are a few questions to consider as we advance through our careers.

1. Who are my key stakeholders?
2. What is important to them?
3. How much power do they have in decision-making?
4. How frequently do they want to be contacted?

5. What method should I use to keep them updated?

When you start in a team lead or manager role, one of your first tasks should be to develop stakeholder maps for your stakeholders. It can be helpful to break the stakeholder maps down into Critical and Important stakeholders, for example, and develop routines for each group according to the questions above.

Effectively managing your stakeholder interactions will determine how successful you are in your role. Failing to deliver for one critical stakeholder can have long-lasting adverse career impacts, especially if it happens more than once.

Know your values

This section could also be labelled "Know what you stand for". Are you an inclusive manager? Do you value diverse thinking styles? Are you a command-and-control manager who believes that all decision-making should happen at the top? Is it essential for you that we treat people fairly? Should integrity and authenticity be part of your management culture? Some organisations talk a good game in this space but don't follow through. If you are a values-driven individual (and all of us should be), an organisation that talks the talk but fails to walk the walk may not be for you. The constant clash between an inauthentic organisational culture and your desire to live according to your values will very likely wear you out.

Your values are the things you believe are fundamental to how you live and work – the definition provided by the Oxford English Dictionary online is "Principles or standards of behaviour; one's judgement of what is important in life."

When we are working in a team or organisation where the culture aligns with our values, we feel like we belong. The work we do may feel more meaningful, and we will be more willing to give personal time to the company or team.

On the other hand, as mentioned above, a poor cultural fit for our value system may make us feel disconnected, and our work may not feel like it has meaning.

This is why it is so essential to understand your values, and how work can help you live them.

Questions that are sometimes given to help identify your values include:

- Identify those times when you were happiest at work or in your personal life. What were you doing? Were you working on your own or with others?
- What were you doing when you were most proud of your accomplishments? E.g. Were you contributing to a personally important cause through volunteering?
- Were there times when you felt particularly fulfilled? If so, what were you doing?

By answering questions like these for yourself, you can narrow down those things that are most important to you. From there you can identify the attributes that describe those values, e.g.

accountability, professionalism, diligence, fairness, integrity, effectiveness.

You can then prioritise what is most important to you, and look for work that helps you develop with those values in mind.

While a lot of our values may be embedded, it is necessary to understand that your values may change over time. As you mature, it may become relevant to you to build an inclusive work culture, for example.

A useful exercise is to detail your top three or five most important values, and then review how your current working environment aligns to them. It can also be helpful to ask yourself if those values represent who you are – are you proud of them? Would you be willing to stand in front of a large group of people at a town hall-style meeting and discuss your values? If I asked a member of your team about your values, would they know what you stand for?

By being true to ourselves and working in line with our values, we will naturally be more authentic. We will also most likely feel fulfilled in our workplaces and will focus on what is important to us.

If we fail to articulate our values and understand why they are relevant to us, we can find ourselves drifting through roles without understanding why we feel dissatisfied or out-of-kilter with the organisation we are working within.

It is also important to note that by understanding our values, we can more easily identify like-minded people with whom we can partner. A small group of people driven by a shared set of values, with a clear goal in mind, can be a tremendous force for positive change. Developing a common value framework has formed the basis for many great companies.

Know your thinking style

Understanding how we think is crucial to understanding how we work, and importantly, how we work with others. It can be very challenging for "creative" people to try to work with "logical" thinkers, or for right and left-brain dominant thinkers to try to understand each other.

In her book "Thriving in Mind", Katherine Benziger discusses a model of the cerebral cortex that takes a quadrant-based approach to classify thinking styles. If you're a frontal-right thinker, for example, you're much more likely to be spontaneous and talk with your hands. If you're a basal or rear-left thinker, you're more oriented to organisation and list-making. This model of thinking styles closely mirrors the various colours-based thinking models (for example, the Green, Blue, Yellow,

Red models, where Green maps to the front-left cortex, Red to the front-right, Yellow to the basal left and Blue to the basal left).

According to Benziger and the models based on her work, we all start with one dominant mode of thinking (we start in one quadrant) but can develop "adjacencies" in other quadrants. Some rare people develop competencies in all four thinking styles and become known as "whole-brain" thinkers. Others will evolve in two, or even three and will be rounder individuals that those with fewer adjacencies. If you're a single quadrant thinker, you're probably in an individual contributor role and will likely remain there for the bulk of your career without development assistance.

I usually start a group mentoring series by doing an exercise with people to have them identify their dominant thinking style by colour. I like this model because Benziger has taken the time to share the neuroscience behind it – when we're thinking in our dominant mode, things come more easily to us. This phenomenon has been demonstrated through functional MRI (fMRI) studies. When we're in the opposite style (e.g. someone with a Blue dominance thinking in a Green manner) it can be very taxing. We're much less efficient and use more glucose and oxygen (fuels for the brain).

There are many different personality and thinking-style classifications out there. The Myers-Briggs Type Indicator, also known as MBTI, is exceptionally well known and is based on the work of psychologist Carl Jung.

There is a simplified MBTI test available at 16 Personalities (http://www.16personalities.com) which is both fun and informative.

Why are thinking and personality types relevant? By understanding how we think and manage ourselves, we are better positioned to understand others as well. If we can identify, for example, that a logical (Green, or frontal-left) thinker likes to have data-driven discussions, it can help us tailor our communications with them to be more successful.

I would suggest this as an exercise for you, the reader, to investigate further. The more we understand ourselves and those we work with, the more successful we will be.

Know your objectives

Ideally, your objectives (or goals) should derive from your values and your organisation's values.

When we think about who those objectives deliver for, in most cases, there should be a customer in mind.

It can be easy to lose sight of the customer you're serving, especially if your role in the organisation is multiple layers away from the end-customer.

Everything we do in a large or small organisation should ultimately be in the interest of the customer. We need to manage by outcomes and ensure that the work we're doing delivers against those outcomes.

There are several ways to approach understanding, setting and tracking your objectives to delivery.

SMART goals are one approach – Specific, Measurable, Achievable, Realistic and Time-bound. This framework encourages the setting of objectives that have more structure than a basic "I want to achieve X" approach.

However, one method for goal-setting that is seeing significant adoption in some of the most successful organisations in multiple fields is the OKR approach, or Objectives and Key Results.

The OKR framework originated under Andy Grove at Intel and is based on the use of aspirational and challenging objectives, managed through specific, measurable and time-bound Key Results.

John Doerr, who worked with Andy Grove at Intel, has written a handy reference called "Measure What Matters". This book provides a gentle introduction to implementing OKRs in your organisation and the necessity of having careful measurements by which to drive your activities.

OKRs don't replace high-level mission and goal setting, but they do provide a mechanism for delivering transparency on progress to those goals. OKRs are intended to be aspirational and inspirational – if your Key Results are too easy to achieve, they won't drive your team and organisation forward in the right way. One way of viewing how inspirational they are is to ask yourself if you were explaining them to a potential new hire, would they be interested in joining your team or company based on the description of your OKRs?

One of my favourite stories about tying your work to an inspirational objective is the (possibly apocryphal) tale of JFK's visit to a NASA facility in 1962. During the tour of the facility, he noticed a janitor carrying a broom. He is said to have stopped his walk, and to have said "Hi, I'm Jack Kennedy. What are you doing?" And the janitor is said to have replied: "Well, Mister President, I'm helping to put a man on the moon."

While the above may or may not have happened, it shows two things – good leadership behaviours (talk with and listen to everyone to understand what is happening in an organisation) and the importance of a clear mission that everyone can get behind.

There's an essential addition to this; in the role of a leader, part of the responsibility is to ensure that everyone understands what the current top priorities are to achieve the organisation's goals. The leader should reiterate the top 2 or 3 (or worst case, 5) priorities consistently until they are complete, and tie them to the overarching objective, in every town hall or all-hands meeting. Managers should cascade those priorities regularly, to the point where people get tired of hearing about them. This kind of communication is never "one and done" – it requires ongoing repetition until everyone in the organisation knows how their work aligns to the current priorities, and how those priorities align to the goals. By consistently doing this, we can give people meaning, which is vital to ensuring that people are engaged to deliver against objectives and come to work with purpose.

Know when to start something

It can sometimes feel that there is never enough time in the day. Human beings are incredible in what we can accomplish. We are also incredible in the way we can procrastinate, and sometimes avoid doing things we know, deep down, we should do.

Zig Ziglar is quoted as saying "You don't have to be great to start, but you have to start to be great." Zig was the precursor to many modern self-help gurus, including Tony Robbins, Tim Ferriss and others. He was a hugely entertaining speaker, who had an exaggerated cadence to his speech, and over-pronounced words for effect. If you watch early YouTube videos of him, you'll see what I mean. He had some very quotable quotes, but more importantly, he shared some very helpful insights about human behaviour, and the one above is a fine example. We have to stop making excuses for ourselves and just start somewhere. Too often we trap ourselves in "analysis paralysis", looking for the perfect time or the right amount of information to make a decision. We may miss opportunities or fail to move forward at all by getting stuck in this pattern.

Jocko Willink, who I quote elsewhere in the book, puts it like this – "Where do you start? Here. And Now."

What does this mean? Get enough resources and information to kick off your project (whether it's a book, or a new website, or a work-related improvement project) and just start doing the work. It's **never** going to be the perfect time. Which means that the perfect time to start is always Now. Stop making excuses, stop undermining yourself, and just get going. You will make mistakes. You will fail. But if you don't start, you will never get anywhere.

(It is equally important to know when to Stop. Don't keep starting things and never finish anything. Be aware of your limits (discussed in a subsequent chapter). Also, be aware of your environment. There are better times to start a work project than others – for example, in many organisations the quietest period of the year is in December. This may represent an opportunity or an additional set of challenges, depending on your organization.)

Know how to delegate

Delegation is a skill that has to be learned. As detailed in Ram Charan's book "The Leadership Pipeline", we may be promoted to team lead or manager because we were excellent individual contributors. We may know how to perform a particular task better than anyone who works for us; that doesn't mean that we should. When you become a team leader, it is critically important that you learn how to leverage other people in the organisation to deliver.

Doing this well is at the heart of proper delegation.

Three things that come to mind when I think about delegation:

- Clearly define what success looks like – the person to whom you are delegating the task should know what a good outcome is.
- Always provide sufficient information to complete the task – the person you're delegating to should be able to do the work without having to either a) guess what comes next or b) continually come back to you for guidance.
- Provide a continual support structure – when you have delegated work, you are still the person accountable for ensuring it gets delivered successfully. This means that, while you have to encourage staff to be independent,

they have to know they can come back to you for clarification if required.

Poor delegation leaves people uncertain, confused and anxious. It also results in less than optimal outcomes for your team. In the next couple of paragraphs, I've described two different aspects of misfiring delegation and ownership.

The Seagull manager

Seagulls are loud, disruptive, and swoop in and out, leaving a mess behind them. Hence, the seagull manager. This kind of management style results in agitation, problems dropped in people's laps, and invariably a mess that needs to be cleaned up.

This kind of "dive-bombing" delegation doesn't work, especially if it is followed up with the harassing behaviour that seagulls are known for conducting. Managers in this category drop off a task, then follow-up with increasingly noisy demands for updates until the work is complete. This style often epitomises micro-management at its worst.

Don't be a seagull manager.

The Monkey Management problem

As a new manager, a core part of your job is to understand what is yours to deliver, and what your staff have to provide on your behalf. This concept was nicely captured in a Harvard Business Review article first published in 1974 and then reprinted in the late 1990s, which described the idea of dropped off problems as monkeys.

While the thrust of the article is how to manage your time as a manager, management of issues is also a critical facet of delegation.

When one of your staff brings a problem to you, your job as a manager is not to take ownership of the problem. Your job is to help your staff member identify how to solve their problem themselves, and not to accumulate other people's problems in your office. If you fail to enable your team, you will become the keeper of your team's monkeys – not a productive situation in which to find yourself.

Rather than spending all of your time on things that are not yours to deliver directly, enable your team to be successful. Support them in understanding what a well-delivered task looks like. Help them with critical thinking when examining problems. Most importantly, praise and reward them for work done well, so they gain confidence. This approach is the management equivalent of "teaching a man to fish". If you catch fish (solve problems) for your staff, they will never become self-sufficient. Teach them how to catch fish, and they can do so in a variety of situations for many different problem species.

Know your numbers

I'm not just referring to operational metrics here. For any manager, knowing your finances is critical. What does your travel and expense budget look like for the year? How would you manage it if your budget gets reduced by 10, 30 or 50%? What do your staff costs look like, and how are you managing them?

These are all valuable figures to have to hand and to have plans to manage. Funding for staff is particularly important and is often driven by factors outside of an early-career manager's ability to control.

Market forces can result in sales downturns, and that in turn can result in cost-reduction challenges being handed down through the organisation. Having contingency plans in place in the event of a 10% challenge to your annual budget is both prudent and regularly required.

There are many budgeting tools available, and your organisation will have its idiosyncrasies in terms of budget cycles (by calendar year? By financial year running from April-April? etc.) and in terms of how those forecasts and budgets are managed.

I have found it very helpful to develop relationships with partners in the Chief Financial Office (CFO) or other financial groups to understand how finances are managed in a particular organisation (e.g. are change and manage budgets different?) so that if you need help, you know where to get it.

From an operational metric point of view (which could be known by any number of three-letter acronyms in your organisation, such as KRIs (Key Risk Indicators), KPIs (Key Performance Indicators), SLAs (Service Level Agreements), etc.) it is critical to know what is fundamental. And then it is vital to only measure and report on those things that are important and relevant. Too often, I've attended management reviews where a presenter shows up with a Powerpoint deck full of metrics, sometimes up to 100 pages long (I kid you not). These are somehow expected to be used to develop an understanding of the current state of play in an organisation or area, usually in a 60-minute meeting.

Don't perpetuate a culture of meaningless metrics. In the section on "Know your Objectives", I mentioned OKRs – this is one way to track progress over a defined period. Solely reporting on Objectives and Key Results may not give your organisation a complete picture, however.

On my blog site, I wrote a post about the madness in perpetuating useless metrics, and the need to be like a gardener, pruning or eliminating those measurements that don't empirically tell you how your organisation is functioning. No-one has enough spare time in their lives to sit through another pointless hour-long meeting.

When presenting metrics, a functioning operational dashboard is self-explanatory. You should be able to provide a single page or slide view to any half-way involved or intelligent senior manager and expect them to understand what the dashboard tells them about the organisation without having to provide a lot of background. This readability requirement means two things – metrics should be labelled clearly, and changes in state (Red/Amber/Green status, for example) should be very clearly called out. If a critical metric is hidden five slides down in the presentation, it's in the wrong place, or it's not the right metric.

(While we're on the subject of Powerpoint, less is more, and always tell a story, as described in the section "Become a storyteller").

Know your strengths

There is a decision to be made when seeking to develop ourselves. Do we focus on our strengths and make them stronger, becoming the best we can be in a narrow range, or do we focus on weaknesses and become more of a generalist?

My position on this is likely to be somewhat unsatisfying – my answer, at least for now, is that "it depends". Traditional coaching mechanisms, at least during my career, have been strength-focussed. That can be fine, depending on what you're doing. For example, if you're a football player (soccer, for those in the US) and you want to become the best goalie you can be, practicing skills that would make you a better striker wouldn't make any sense.

On the other hand, if your weaknesses are likely to impact your ability to do your day job (for example, you lack emotional intelligence, but want to be a good people manager), then it might be worth developing those weaknesses to at least raise your baseline level of competence.

To make your decision as to what is relevant at a point in time, you need to understand your role, as described in a previous chapter, but also, more importantly, you need to know your strengths and weaknesses.

Getting to know your strengths isn't solely a matter for introspection. Many tools exist that will help you map out what your strongest capabilities are (www.mindtools.com, for example), but if you rely on those alone, your own biases may come in to play. It makes sense to get feedback from people around you to help you map out your strengths. In a corporate situation, tools like 360 feedback systems can be beneficial, depending on the believability of those who provide feedback.

A 360 process allows your manager, peers, direct reports and usually customers to provide anonymised feedback to you. This process can be a bruising experience if you haven't gone through it before, but it can also be an excellent way to gain insights into how you are perceived. Most of the tools I've used present the results in a map that compares how you've rated yourself against the average view of how your respondents have rated you. Mapping of this kind can be a practical way to identify areas where you have hidden weaknesses or strengths. The key thing to understand about 360 feedback is that it focusses more on behavioural competencies rather than technical, and is not delivery-focussed in most cases.

Mentors can be a helpful way of developing an unbiased understanding of your strengths, and coaches can be beneficial in developing them further. (I won't go into a lot of detail on the differences between mentors and coaches here, but I usually think of coaches as being helpful for skills-based support, similar to a defensive or offensive coach in various sports. Mentors are often more useful for helping to develop networks, or plan your next career move.)

If you choose to focus on developing strengths further, how do you decide which ones to grow? Again, I think the answer changes depending on what is relevant to your role and organisation at a point in time. If you are going through a significant organisational change, and you are good at planning and managing organisational transformation, volunteering to help drive aspects of the transformational program can help develop critical skills further.

If you choose to focus on weaknesses, it is necessary to decide how far you want to take your skills development. I could do online courses and practice coding until the universe ends, and I will never be much of a software developer. While it might be worth my while to develop competencies in this area to understand, for example, how an Agile development process works, it will not be a good use of my time to try to become competent in Java.

How do you know if you're working in an area of strength or weakness? When we are doing something we are naturally good at, there is a sense of ease – and sometimes, joy. Using strengths doesn't feel forced – we don't feel like we're pushing against internal blockages simply to move the needle. There is a neurobiological basis for this. When we discussed thinking styles earlier, I mentioned that operating in a thinking framework that isn't central to us *feels* more taxing *because it is*. We use more mental effort (and oxygen and glucose) when we're doing something that isn't in our core strengths. The opposite is the feeling of flow we get when we do something that we're naturally good at. Some people are natural orators and revel in the attention of a crowded room. Appropriate words come to them as if by magic, and they feel energised by the experience of an active Q&A. For others, this is their idea of a perfect hell.

On the subject of introverted leaders, I recently participated in a quarterly discussion of senior regional talent that my organisation is looking to develop. One of the individuals we discussed is well known for his excellent service delivery, his relationships with the business, and his subject matter expertise. His level of introversion renders him almost mute in a group setting, however. When I raised that as a possible development area, particularly concerning him promoting ideas at an all-hands meeting, for example, one of my colleagues rightly (and politely) corrected me. He reminded me that diversity of thought and approach are equally important when it comes to leading organisations and that this individual's strengths far outweighed his weakness. To get him to focus on developing his weaker areas would have been a waste of time, and a disincentive to him.

Consider that for yourselves; only you can determine which strengths and weaknesses you should focus on developing. Before that, you have to put in the time to get to know them.

Know your limits

When we are looking at what we're able to commit to it is vitally important to know where our capabilities begin and end, and also to understand how far we can successfully push ourselves.

Sometimes limits can only be found by testing ourselves (or a system) to failure, but we can often observe signs of impending disaster before an actual failure takes place. For example, if we find we're overloaded because we've committed to too much, and critical deliverables are starting to slip, it's probably time to raise a hand and ask for help.

At times it's also possible to overestimate our knowledge and to extend ourselves into spaces where we are operating beyond our limits. Again, this can be an opportunity for growth, but overextending too far can lead to failure or even disaster.

If we are not subject matter experts, it is often better to ask questions rather than make statements. By putting ourselves in a "student" frame of mind, we're more likely to expand our limits through learning. By assuming we know something, we're less open. We may then find the limits of our knowledge through failure rather than through questioning someone who is a subject matter expert.

On the subject of physical and mental limits, I had the privilege of working with a highly dedicated, very driven individual. He was always available to assist with work-related issues, no matter the hour. On one occasion, we were on an incident management call, and he had been working long hours for several weeks. While we were talking, he said: "That's strange...my hands are starting to swell.". He then went on to report other symptoms. I recommended that he drop from the call and seek medical attention, which he reluctantly did.

It turned out that his liver was failing as the result of an infection. His body had been so stressed for so long that he was unable to fight the infection normally, and he was admitted to hospital. He was critically ill at one point. He has a young family, and could well have died. He subsequently began working for me, and one of our regular checkpoint questions was how many hours he was working and whether he was being conscientious about looking after his health.

My message to him has been that we need to know our limits and live within them. No matter how seemingly important your job is, it is just a job. Most of us are trying to serve customers, not save lives (which does, necessarily, change the equation). Your family need you to be around for them, and working yourself to death won't help them one bit.

Know your organisation

Organisations come in all shapes and sizes, with all kinds of cultures. Whether you're working in a 2-person start-up or a 200,000-person corporation, some things make that organisation culturally unique. All companies are a combination of culture and people, as Ray Dalio describes wonderfully in his book "Principles".

Not-for-profit and volunteering organisations may have different cultural values and attributes compared to commercial organisations. A school will behave differently to a hospital. The departments will be labelled similarly but may have different ways of operating.

Whenever you join a new organisation, understanding your place in it can be tricky. As described in "Know your role", it's imperative to determine where your team sits in the value chain. Understanding this helps you to comprehend how your group depends on inputs from other teams and how your outputs feed other parts of the organisation.

Developing an understanding of the organisation's values is something that shouldn't wait until you've joined a new company. You should know what a company stands for before you decide whether you're going to work for it. That said, the publicly-communicated values and how the company operates may not align – and as discussed previously, this cultural dissonance can create significant challenges.

Learn as much as you can about the company culture as soon as you can, and then immerse yourself in it if it is the right cultural fit for you (if not, you may not have done sufficient homework).

Find out which groups or departments are essential to your deliverables. For example, if you are part of a customer-facing technology organisation, what teams do you depend on to deliver for your customers? If you're in Software Engineering, are you dependent on

Infrastructure teams to ensure products get delivered on time to new customers?

In addition to learning your new role, you need to build mental maps of the organisation as you become part of it. These mental maps can help inform your networking efforts as you learn who you need to partner with.

If you think of those groups you are immediately connected to as your "neighbourhood map", this is the area of the organisation that you will develop the most in-depth and most effective understanding of. Beyond the neighbourhood, there may be a regional view that is important, depending on the scale of the organisation. And beyond that, the organisation may be global.

Groups that are not in your neighbourhood may still impact your ability to deliver. For example, HR and Finance are typically "global map" groups. In a medium-large organisation, they will have a lot of power in terms of hiring ability and decision-making on certain investments.

It is crucial to know some parts of the global map better than others for this reason. If your company has a Compliance or Legal department, you may only interact with them when there is a particular, very occasional query. It is still important to know what they are responsible for in general terms, and how their work impacts yours (and vice versa).

Apart from the internal process of mapping the organisation, it is also helpful to understand what your company stands for so that you can tell other people. Senior managers from any company will be able to tell you about the values that drive the company, the culture within it, as well as the economic outlook and the challenges the company faces.

As a junior manager, developing an understanding of these topics can not only make you feel more connected to the organisation you work for but can also help you understand how your work benefits the organisation and its goals.

Key to any organisation of any size is the people within it. As part of building stakeholder maps and networking, you will develop connections with the right people in the organisation to help move your goals forward. Failing to understand who these people are will result in poor outcomes for you and your teams.

Know your industry

Learning about the best practices and successful approaches in your industry, be that technology, financial services, pharmaceutical, non-profit or otherwise can help you be more successful and provide valuable insights inside your organisation. In vast enterprises, it can often be challenging to develop a practice of learning about your competitors and the space in which your organisation operates, but it does convey an advantage to managers willing to make an effort.

Of course, there are industries where one requires detailed knowledge to function – for example, in highly regulated areas like healthcare and financial services, almost everyone in any role is expected to have a basic understanding of core regulations to be compliant. There is more to it than this, though. Attending industry conferences can, for example, expose you to peers doing a similar job but in a different way, potentially helping to shape your thinking. Knowing who your counterparts are in several competitor organisations can be useful to triangulate on approaches to common problems. Additionally, understanding where success and failure have been rewarded or punished from a market perspective can inform those strategies that your company or enterprise adopts.

By taking the time to read relevant industry publications, attend conferences, talk with vendors and meet with peers, you can significantly increase the value of the overall "knowledge package" that you bring to your organisation. This awareness, can, in turn, help you with career development and with building networks of like-minded peers in and outside your organisation.

Know how to manage conflict
Conflict makes many of us deeply uncomfortable. The behaviours we can engage in just to avoid conflict would be amusing if it weren't for their potential impact.

Conflict is inevitable. This doesn't make it good or bad – how it is handled is what matters. Whether at the nation-state or individual level, the reasons humans engage in conflict are many.

Here are just a few:

- Different value and/or belief systems
- Different views of reality – again inevitable, since we all perceive reality differently
- Competition for resources
- As a response to perceived or actual interference
- Differences of opinion (related to different views of reality)
- Communication gaps and/or misunderstandings
- Bullying and/or harassment

There are others, particularly in the workplace.

We have several approaches that we can take to deal with conflict, whether directly involving ourselves or as a mediator between others.

Avoidance – ignoring or avoiding conflict is the equivalent of sticking your head in the sand. It's not going to improve the situation.

Management – understanding the causes of conflict, and then working with the individuals involved to manage towards a successful resolution is a vital skill for any leader. Some tactics for managing conflict are:

- Set ground rules for acceptable behaviours when discussing the source of conflict
- Deal with the source of the issue in a head-on, but respectful way
- Reserve debate for the things that really matter. Constant conflict is draining and can distract from the business at hand.
- Look for the best possible outcome from the situation.

Advantage – using conflict as a way to move your agenda forward is something that can only be achieved if you have strategies for managing it.

All functional leadership teams that I have been part of have worked through conflict to be successful. The best teams have engaged in strong (but not vicious) debate in order to work through differences.

Learning to manage conflict and use it to advantage when appropriate (to surface critical issues, for example) is a vital skillset. Don't ignore or avoid it, because you will miss opportunities to identify and deal with substantive issues that could be impacting you or your organisation's performance.

Embrace conflict in a positive way.

Know what you don't know

In several sections in this book, I will talk about the importance of humility, directly or indirectly. When we're young, we may not think that we know it all, but we certainly believe we know more than we do. As we gain in age and experience, we become ever more aware of how much we don't know. It helps us stay grounded, even if we're very successful. It helps us to listen when others are talking. It helps us to question the established orthodoxy, when necessary. And it helps us to identify areas of development, for ourselves and our organisations.

When we deeply "know" something, we stop questioning it. Thirty years ago, people knew that computers would never beat people at chess until IBM's Deep Blue soundly defeated Gary Kasparov in 1996. Until the 16th century, scientists and astronomers "knew" that the Earth was the centre of the Universe. It was only in the 17th century that Kepler's heliocentric model with elliptical orbits replaced the geocentric model, which then became the accepted pattern for planetary movement.

Until quite recently, we "knew" that we had a single, indivisible self in our heads, and that we humans are distinct from animals because of free will. In recent times we've discovered that free will is open to question – for example, Yuval Noah Harari's book, "Homo Deus", postulates that we are biological automata. We are driven by a series of neurological cascades, which we have no control over, nor direct knowledge of. If you've ever decided to "not think" to exercise your free will, see what happens. Besides, our left and right brains, if disconnected from each other due to trauma, act almost independently – there are some fascinating cases in medical literature around this.

So, a lot of what we "know" should be open to question. We should understand that things we think are immutable may actually be subject to change. We may confuse assumptions with knowledge and fail to validate our thinking. By being willing to question ourselves, and others, we learn more about the possible reality we are inhabiting. Most of us don't have the time to apply a rigorous scientific method to our daily thoughts and decisions, but we should be willing to think more before assuming we know something. By doing this in front of our teams, and being ready to have dialogue, we also make it safe for our teams to question us and each other in a constructive manner.

Manage

The following sections are elements of how to manage ourselves, our teams and our careers. They are not intended to be comprehensive, but to give pointers to areas where a bit of focus can help developing managers move forward (and we should all be developing continuously).

There is a wealth of resources available, from books to YouTube videos to blog posts on these (and many other management) topics. I've recommended a few books in the text but will include a list in the Bibliography section.

Learn what works for you in terms of your style and your preferred method of learning. Develop a practice of improving your management style, taking feedback from others as you go. And most importantly, be intentional about managing your time, your health and your processes.

Manage your time

Each day we are granted 24 hours to do with as we wish. Taking the recommended 8 hours for sleep leaves us with 16. Most of us spend at least 9 hours in our workplace – this is plenty of time to accomplish a significant amount if we choose to spend it wisely.

In his letters to Lucilius, Seneca the Younger wrote:

"Therefore, Lucilius, do as you write me that you are doing: hold every hour in your grasp. Lay hold of today's task, and you will not need to depend so much upon tomorrow's. While we are postponing, life speeds by."

Seneca wrote those words sometime around 63-65AD, and they are still true today.

Our challenges come from our "distractible" nature, and the vast number of distractions that present themselves to us. For every interruption in our current task, researches estimate that it can take 25 minutes to get back on track. If you are in the middle of preparing a presentation, for example, responding to an email alert, or a text message, or having a colleague drop by, doesn't just cost you the time of the interruption itself – it is that time, plus the reset time your brain requires to get back on task.

Blocking out time to work on projects, or to think, or to spend time learning, is vital to preventing time being frittered away on non-essential items.

Carving out time for less critical, but still urgent, tasks is also hugely important. Many books on time management recommend setting specific times during the day for email management, for example. If you get into a routine in this area and set expectations appropriately with people who contact you by email, you can reduce the distraction caused by it significantly.

There is a rating system that is attributed to General Dwight D. Eisenhower, appropriately called the Eisenhower matrix. It breaks tasks down by Urgency and Importance.

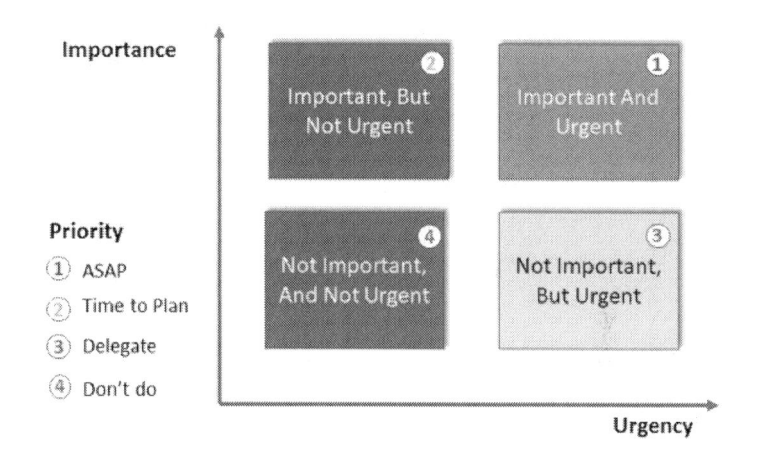

	Important, But Not Urgent ②	Important And Urgent ①
	Not Important, And Not Urgent ④	Not Important, But Urgent ③

Importance (vertical axis), Urgency (horizontal axis)

Priority
① ASAP
② Time to Plan
③ Delegate
④ Don't do

Activities that are both Urgent and Important represent the top priority. On the other hand, tasks that are non-Urgent and not Important should probably never get done.

Most of us spend time on tasks in the bottom category, unless we focus on how we manage our time, and develop task lists during the day that bubble up the critical items to the top.

Another tool in the arsenal of successful time managers is the ability to say "No". A lot of us are not very practised at this, and it causes us to take on more work than we can successfully deliver. This unwillingness could be due to fear of missing out (FOMO), or concern that we might hurt someone's feelings if we chose not to mentor them, for example.

The challenge is to identify those items that we can say "Yes" to and ensure we can deliver successfully by appropriately setting expectations.

Time planning

There are plenty of ways in which you could organise your day, and many books written on the subject. The most effective way will vary from individual to individual and will differ at different stages of your career.

Here are a few golden rules:

- Protect time for learning. If you're not learning, you're stagnating. Do that for too long, and you will lose relevance to your organisation and hurt your career.
- Use your time of highest productivity for your most challenging tasks. All of us have times

when we are more focussed and more tuned in. The times when you are most productive may well change as you age. I do most of my heaviest lifting in the early afternoon, but I'm aware that early morning (before 7:30) is when I'm least distracted.
- Develop a planning mechanism for tasks and projects, and use it religiously. Building time management habits takes time, ironically, but it is time well spent. Habitual time management makes us more productive.
- Make it clear when you cannot be disturbed. If you're working on a high-value task, don't let lower value interruptions, e.g. email, chat messages, disrupt you and take you off track.

Help your team develop good practices as well, and you will all be more productive. If your team know you will be available at specific times for clinics (in my current organisation we use 10@10, or 10 minutes at 10 am, as an example) then they will prepare themselves for those times.

The more you practice planning and time management, the more instinctual it becomes. People will appreciate you being transparent and organised, and the volume of your output will increase.

Manage your energy

Most of us have ebbs and flows in our energy levels. (There are apparent exceptions – those people who seem to be "always-on" – but I would suggest that even these exceptional people also have peaks and troughs in energy levels, although at a less extreme level.) Drops in energy can be point-in-time, due to illness, for example, or longer-term caused by lack of sleep or overwork. There are also ebbs and flows during our day.

It is necessary to understand when your energy levels are highest so that you can target those times for your most demanding work. For example, I know I do my best thinking before lunchtime, so I spend time developing goals, or working on strategy during that time of day. I know that I'm prone to lower energy levels in the late afternoon and early evening, so I handle more routine tasks then, like catching up on email.

There are also seasonal peaks and troughs in energy for some people. I met a friend of mine recently who is an incredibly high-energy person, and she told me that she struggles in the Winter. While she doesn't believe she has Seasonal Affective Disorder, she has noticed that her energy levels are much lower in the Winter than when the days are longer.

Our energy levels can peak and drop through our careers as well. This pattern is also important to recognise, because if you're in a role where the organisation is requiring less of you at a point when your energy levels are particularly high, you may become frustrated. High-energy periods may be times to consider looking for a more significant role or looking at moving to a new organisation. Additionally, it is essential to recognise that when your energy levels are consistently low (for example, after the birth of a child), there is no shame in taking on a less challenging project or role until you rebound.

Recognise those times in your life when you have a lot of energy, and seek to direct that energy towards positive outcomes. And secondly, be aware when you are at a low ebb, and be kind to yourself. Try to find things that you can do at those times that don't require the highest energy version of you to be successful. I suspect we all have those times, and part of being productive is identifying those times when you are at your most energetic and looking to increase your output accordingly.

Manage your focus

I read somewhere once that what gets focussed on gets attended to. In simple terms, what this means is that the things on which we choose to concentrate will get "front of brain" time. There's an excellent example of this called the "Selective Attention Test" (also known as the Monkey Business Illusion), which is available on Youtube. Born out of research from Daniel Simons and Christopher Chabris, the study shows what happens when we focus the majority of our attention on one aspect of a moving scene. I won't spoil the surprise if you haven't seen this, but here's a test you can try yourself.

If you have a group of people in a room with you, give them 30 seconds to note all of the things that are brown (or black or blue, or whatever) in the office or outside. After the time is up, get them to tell you how many red objects they saw. Because of the way our brain applies selective attention, they will be able to tell you about far fewer red objects than if they had been asked to focus on red objects from the start.

Why is this important in a work context? Here's an example. If we tell people to focus exclusively on one type of customer or availability metric, that is what will drive their activities. A poorly constructed measurement will incentivise the wrong behaviour and may cause attentional blindness to something far more critical. For example, if someone in a retail context is incentivised to focus on number of customers served per shift or per hour, they may be abrupt and brusque with customers in order to "achieve their target", rather than focussing on customer satisfaction, which in most cases is far more likely to result in repeat business.

There's a chain of grocery stores in the US called Trader Joe's, which has built up a cult following over the years. Fans of the chain often create online petitions to bring a Trader Joe's to their city or state, because they have experienced it elsewhere. The chain operates in a very different fashion to the more substantial players in the market, like Walmart or Kroger. It focusses on creating customer experiences. There's a fascinating podcast on the topic (Freakonomics Radio, Episode 359 – "Should America be Run by Trader Joe's?"). One of the key things that struck me about it was how the chain encourages their staff (crew members, in Trader Joe-speak) to focus on delighting customers. Regardless of whatever else is going on in a store, if a crew member spends 15 minutes finding a single $5 bottle of wine for an individual customer, that is time well spent. The metric driving customer behaviour is demonstrably not speed of interaction – it is some variant of "number of happy customers". Crew members also stock the shelves of the store during the working day, something that the majority of grocery chains do not do. This practice intends to encourage customer interactions – Trader Joe's hires staff for their outgoing and engaging personalities to strengthen this practice. The result is not only a retail chain with a devoted fan base; it has the highest sales per square footage metric of any grocery chain in the United States.

We can attribute this success (at least in part) to where the management of Trader Joe's choose to focus the attention of their staff.

In our working and personal lives, managing our focus can be challenging. Interruptions during the working day can have knock-on implications for work that requires sustained focus. Energy levels, discussed in a previous chapter, can also impact our ability to pay attention to high impact work, as can a lack of sleep. Several things can be done to improve the ability to focus at work:

1. Minimise interruptions, when high-quality attention is needed, such as when doing strategic planning or focussed critical thinking.
2. If working with others on this particular piece of work, encourage people to be present in the room by banning phones, tablets and laptops except at set break times.
3. Use meditation to improve focus. Practising meditation doesn't work for everyone, but 10 minutes of mindfulness practice performed regularly has been shown to improve mental focus by altering brain function.
4. Document the goals or outcomes that need to be delivered from the session, and bring the focus back to those if you or the other participants start to wander off-topic.
5. Repeat the agreed steps to achieve the goals to ensure that you collectively understand what was accepted, and cement focus on those actions.
6. Take breaks regularly. It has been postulated that the longest that people can maintain a sustained focus on mentally-demanding tasks is approximately 20 minutes. This amount of time is believed to be decreasing, due to the impact

of social media, television and the whirl of modern life.

Focus is vital to ensuring that the right things get done. By making it clear what needs our attention (what our goals are) and applying focus to those, we significantly increase the likelihood of successfully delivering against our objectives.

Manage your health

The current generation has the benefit of medical science and knowledge that was not available when I was young. Back then, when dinosaurs roamed the earth, we didn't need to worry about the impact of screen time on developing minds, for example. Obesity was almost unheard of in the Ireland I grew up in during the early 70's – we were a poor country then, food was sometimes in short supply, and we spent a lot of time outdoors cycling or running through fields or playing physical games. Life is much more sedentary now. Office hours are longer, and commute times are ever more painful in cities across the world as the earth becomes more populated, and people move to urban areas.

We know now that this lifestyle is bad for us. We eat highly calorific food at times when we can't possibly work it off. We spend more time sitting than any previous generation. Our work is less physically demanding, as many of us in the developed world are knowledge workers, or otherwise office-based. In factories and warehouses, heavy lifting is now done more often by machines than humans.

Sitting is now described as the new smoking. The posture we adopt while sitting at a desk shortens our hip-flexors, reduces our core strength and causes weakening of our back muscles. I have personally had two spinal surgeries, and the first surgeon I went to told me that he had performed more lower lumbar spinal surgeries on people in their 30s than ever before – mostly on people who worked at desks all day. Here are some thoughts on what I think you should consider.

Physical Health.

My number one piece of advice for an office-based worker - get a sit/stand desk if you can. The ability to change your posture during the day helps to lengthen muscles and reduce the impact of hunching over a keyboard. Various studies have also shown that standing burns more calories than sitting, and increases the levels of oxygen in the brain, helping you be more alert.

Make time for exercise. When I travel, I get up early, typically around 5:30 am, and go to the hotel gym. I get the blood pumping around my body and start my day more alert as a result. I also exercise in a fasted state, which helps me control my weight – an ongoing challenge when eating out a lot when on work trips.

If you can't exercise in the morning (and I can't, when I'm not travelling), make time during the day or in the evening. You're going to be more tired in the evening, but it is still possible to get a good workout in – you simply have to make a habit of it, and be disciplined.

If you're not a gym person, pick an exercise that suits you and build it into your routines. The benefits of exercise have been documented for decades and go beyond improving your cardiovascular health.

If you're physically fit, you will be less prone to illness, and you will be a better manager.

Sleep

I have been very sleep-deprived at different points in my life, and it doesn't take a genius to know that a lack of sleep has a direct, negative impact on your performance. My youngest daughter woke approximately 20 times a night for her first two years. Trying to operate on less than 4 hours a night for long periods makes for a grumpy individual and a suboptimal management outlook. As with exercise, the benefits (and necessity) of good sleep patterns have been documented for a very long time. If you have any doubts on this score, I'd recommend doing some research online – there is a vast amount of information available.

While some people can get by with little sleep (5 hours or so), many studies recommend* that we aim for 7-8 hours per night. Sometimes this requires a bit of planning. For example, if you intend to get up early to work out, or you want to commute earlier to beat traffic, you have to go to bed earlier at night (obvious, right?). Jocko Willink, in his book "Discipline Equals Freedom: Field Manual", lays out the steps he puts in place to make sure he sticks to his routine, which involves getting up at 4:30 every morning (Saturday and Sunday included). One key point he makes is that consistency is vital in building good sleep habits.

Quality of sleep is influenced by how late we eat, what kind of food we eat before bed, the lighting and sound in our room, absence of technology, etc., etc. It is an area with a vast amount of study behind it, and I won't even attempt to replicate that research here. Suffice it to say that we need to be more intentional when it comes to sleep to get the best outcomes.

Sleep is used by our bodies to do repair work, to burn fat, and to declutter our minds - among many other physiological and psychological processes.

Prioritise sleep ahead of that last drink, or an episode of Game of Thrones™. It's worth it in the long run, not just from a mental alertness perspective, but also from the point of view of your overall health.

Good quality sleep will set you up to make better decisions, have better interactions, and overall be a better manager to your staff.

Mental Health

At various points in our lives, we may all deal with mental health challenges. Mental health is often used just to refer to adverse conditions such as depression, but it, like physical health, is a set of states, many of which are within our control.

It is essential to build routines to maintain good mental health. Unless we are mindful of our health overall, we can slip into bad habits, or become overwhelmed by circumstances.

I've covered two key elements that support mental health above – sleep and exercise. A lack in either or both of those areas can negatively impact your mental health.

I've outlined some additional suggested activities or routines to support good mental health below:

- Meditate. I've written about this elsewhere in the book, but whether you're meditating for focus, or to reduce stress, I've found it to be a great way to help reset my head. There is plenty of research available to suggest that a meditation practice has health benefits, and I would strongly recommend you give it a try.
- Build meaningful relationships. Having a place in the world that requires us to think beyond ourselves, to help others and to be mindful that everyone has baggage and everyone needs help

can be beneficial to mental health. Having supportive relationships around us is vital to surviving life, which can be pretty bruising at times.
- Manage stress. While a certain amount of pressure is vital to help drive us to develop, too much can be crippling, and can lead to long-term physical and mental health issues. I cover this in more detail in the section "Be resilient".
- Learn to detach from work. At various points in my career, work has woken me from sleep. Sometimes I will have to get out of bed wherever I am and go and write something down because I have to get it out of my head. While work is important, when it is waking you up at night, or keeping you from sleeping, it is clearly out of balance, and you need to find ways to address that. Sometimes hiring or appointing a reliable second-in-command can help, for example. At this stage of my life, when I go on holidays, I check my work phone every 3-4 days, and the rest of the time I leave it locked in my rental accommodation. A few select people know that they can call me on my personal cellphone in case of emergency. I also take two weeks off at Christmas to spend with my children, because this is the most important time of the year for them.
- Examine your mistakes when they happen, learn from them, and then let them go. Keep

the lessons, but not the sense of failure. Dragging around a mental suitcase full of regret is unhelpful for our mental equilibrium, sense of self and self-worth.
- Get a mentor. The ability to have a sounding board to help you develop your thinking, or to help you unravel a particularly tricky problem, can be beneficial and can be supportive of good mental health.
- Talk to a professional. If things are really getting on top of you, and you find that your mental state is not in the best shape, talk to a counsellor or therapist. Many larger organisations provide access to counsellors as part of Employee Assistance Programs, sometimes as a free benefit.

These are just some brief suggestions, which I have found helpful at different times. Develop your own, and evolve them over time. If you're not in the right place mentally, it makes it harder to be the supporter and leader for your team or organisation.

Manage your people

One of the most challenging, but rewarding aspects of becoming a team lead or a new manager is the shift from managing yourself and your output to motivating and managing others. People management is a vast topic area, but because this is intentionally a "short book", I'm going to skim through some high-level thoughts on this.

There are many books written on the subject of people management – I often mention Jo Owens "How to Manage" and "How to Lead" as ones that I recommend, but the management section on Amazon is full to bursting point with books in this category, and new ones are continually being added.

My personal experience is that managing people is about understanding your style and theirs, and making sure you tailor your approach wherever necessary to get the best out of all the people in your team. The US Army Field Manual FM100-5 states, "Leadership is based on knowledge of men." In other words, you have to know your people in to be able to lead and manage them effectively.

Style can be about how you communicate, but it is also to do with how you approach problems, whether you are a micro- or macro-level manager (it's sometimes necessary to fluctuate between the two levels), whether you absorb information by reading or listening, etc.

Stephen Covey, in his "The Seven Habits of Highly Effective People" has as Habit #5 "Seek First to Understand, Then to be Understood".

Understanding individuals (their preferences, values, energy levels and personal lives) is a critical part of trying to manage and motivate people on your team.

We need to develop good listening habits and question when we don't understand. It is sometimes the case that managers do not want to admit they don't understand something for fear of appearing weak or foolish. It is far worse to pretend to understand and to move forward on that basis than it is to question and develop understanding. Your people will respect you for having the humility to ask genuine questions in the effort to establish a shared understanding of any topic.

By being empathetic, and treating your people as people (again, a piece of advice I give regularly – treat everyone as a person first), you will learn about what is essential to your team members and will genuinely connect with them. In an interview with Tony Robbins, Danny Meyer, the CEO of Union Square Hospitality, put it this way – everyone has an invisible sign around their necks that says "Make me feel I'm important." This desire is true for customers, staff, friends and family. Everyone wants to feel that they are relevant in some way. We show our team this by treating them fairly, understanding what motivates them, providing them with the opportunity for growth, and paying attention to them when they are giving us information or asking for assistance.

One practical way that you can help your staff is to ensure that everyone has a development plan. Many organisations provide HR-provided tools to log development plans and opportunities for employees. It is important to note that the development plan is the responsibility of the individual staff member, not the manager. Your role is to help your staff identify what it is they want to develop and then provide them with space and time to do it.

Development plans need to be intentional. It's not enough for someone to say that they want to learn "skill x", or achieve some certification or other, although those may be part of a development plan. If one of your staff is interested in becoming a manager, for example, you need to be precise about the development steps they need to go through to go down that path.

Development plans should be action-oriented, time-bound and achievable. Unlike annual performance reviews, they may be multi-year. Part of our role in providing support to development is to enable people to fail gracefully and learn; provide introductions to mentors or coaches; provide time in the week for targeted learning, and be available for advice and support.

In my opinion, helping people to achieve their full potential is the primary role for any people manager.

We need to put the time in and make the space for people to do that.

Manage your communications

The use of language is a tricky thing, particularly in a multi-country or global organisation. I worked in an 80,000-person company at one point (not the largest one I've worked at), and I had a reasonably sized team based in several locations in India. One of my top Middleware support engineers had been part of the team for around five years, and we spoke reasonably regularly. He was a friendly, positive guy, and I enjoyed working with him. On the day that I left the company, he finally told me that I had been calling him the wrong name for five years. He was in our HR system with his first name and surname in reverse order, and everyone, myself included, had been calling him by his surname for the whole time he worked in the team. He was too polite to say anything.

Because of the cultural differences involved in managing resources in another country, I hadn't recognised the fact that in his part of the world a patronymic was used first in official documentation, followed by a given name. Not my proudest moment, but a good learning experience.

While the above example is more about understanding cultural nuance, it is an example of a communication gap.

The three most common forms of communication used by managers and staff in the organisations I've worked in are email, instant messaging and verbal communications (one-to-one, or one-to-many).

Email

Email is a tricky medium in which to get communications right. As a communication mechanism, email doesn't convey nuance. You don't know if a comment is sarcastic or genuine, and have to make assumptions of intent if the communicator isn't completely clear. You will also have to include additional, external cues based on the individual communicating.

My view is that email communication is a form of tax we pay for working in any large organisation. It drops other people's problems in your world, often without context or courtesy. With that as a backdrop, here are some thoughts on how I believe we should communicate via email.

1. Keep email volume to a minimum wherever possible. We all get too much of it, it is hampered by the points I made above, and every email read is a distraction from a higher-value task. Resetting our brains from an email or other interruption can take between 25-40 minutes.
2. Be as brief as possible in your emails while conveying the message clearly. Spend a bit of

time thinking about what you want to communicate, and then do it concisely and crisply.
3. Don't get into multi-level email chain conversations. These are a massive waste of everyone's time, and often suck in innocent bystanders who then have to try and figure out whether they have a role to play in the unfolding disaster. I have a very low tolerance for people forwarding me email chains that are 7-8 layers deep, and asking me to read from the bottom up. If you can't convey your message or accomplish your goal in one or at most two exchanges, pick up the phone or set up an in-person discussion.
4. Consider adopting a precise tagging mechanism so that the intent of the email is clear immediately to the reader. There is a system which is known as BLUF, or Bottom Line Up Front, that states clearly whether the intention of the email is to ask for help, requires a response, or is just for information. It originated in the US Army, where the need to communicate critical messages at the top of any communication is a way of life (and can help avoid confusion which can lead to life or death consequences).
5. Check your emails before you send them. Too often, simple errors can drastically alter the meaning of a message and can cause confusion

or issues with execution. Also, make sure your recipient list is correct and complete.
6. Be courteous. It costs very little to start an email with a salutation ("Hi, Bob" is enough in most cases, assuming you are communicating with Bob), and finish with a sign-off (e.g. Regards, Kind Regards, Cheers, or whatever is culturally appropriate for you and your organisation). If you keep your emails to a minimum, you won't mind the extra characters required to be polite.
7. I genuinely hadn't realised how irritating I find email until I wrote this down ☐

Instant messaging or Chat

Every organisation I've worked in has had some form of Instant Messaging client, which is widely used (e.g. Skype, Slack, Lotus Notes). Instant messaging is fantastic for fast, informal communication. It helps with the rapid dissemination of information and is particularly useful for getting quick answers to questions from people in your corporate network. However, the informal nature of the medium can be a blessing and a curse.

We may also use some form of chat client in our personal lives, such as WhatsApp. Where problems can creep in is where we fail to segregate our behaviour between personal and corporate environments.

Every organisation I've worked in has had occasional problems with people using corporate chat environments to use inappropriate language, or to share things that are best left outside the workplace. Unsuitable content can run the gamut from swearing (which may be accepted up to a point in your corporate culture, but tends to give an unprofessional impression) to sharing NSFW (Not Suitable For Work) material such as controversial memes or nude pictures. Most large organisations have filters in place to prevent the abuse of the platform, but be aware that the responsibility to understand what is appropriate for our workplaces lies with each of us.

There are a few guidelines I keep in mind for myself (and your organisation will have its own codes of conduct for what is appropriate).

1. Don't write anything about anyone you wouldn't say to their face, or that you would be uncomfortable seeing on the front page of a newspaper with your name attached to it.
2. Set an example for your team as to what is appropriate. Be positive in your communications.
3. Don't use IM as a replacement for personal interaction. It can feel tremendously comfortable to stay at our desks all day and try to run our teams using chat systems.
4. Don't put confidential information in a chat window.

5. Avoid discussing topics that may make members of your team or other people in the company uncomfortable.
6. Be courteous. In the same way that courtesy goes a long way in email, it does so in IM. If you're connecting with someone for the first time via IM, give them some context as to who you are, particularly if you work in a large or very substantial organisation.

It's easy to forget that internal chat communications are often monitored, and if you work in a regulated industry (e.g. Finance, HealthCare, Pharmaceutical) they may also be discoverable by regulators. In addition, things that are expected to stay within a company's four walls can find their way outside, if people within the company feel strongly enough about sharing them with the world. Be prepared to stand behind what you write, and assume that it is already in the public record.

Verbal communication

There are many ways in which we can verbally communicate with our staff, peers and partners, from phone calls to in-person chats to more formal meetings and town-hall-style presentations.

The formality and content of spoken communication will vary based on the context. As with the other forms of communication mentioned above, it is vital to know what we're trying to communicate, who our audience is, and how we can most effectively get our message across.

I've listed a few points that may help with verbal communication below.

1. Listen first. Understand your audience, and what they're interested in. If you're in a one-to-one conversation, don't rush in to answer – give your partner in the discussion the opportunity to get their message across first.
2. Think about what you want to say before you speak. The adage of being better to be thought a fool than open our mouths and removing all doubt has a lot of truth. When I'm speaking in public, particularly to large groups, and it's off the cuff, I take the time to order my thoughts before I discuss a point or answer a question. When I'm mentoring people who are new to speaking to their teams or larger groups, I use the analogy of a train. If you get the train cars aligned in your head and know the order they're in then it is easier to stay on message.
3. Be as brief as is reasonable. Brevity is an under-appreciated skill, and for those of us who have kissed the Blarney Stone, it is one that we don't exercise often enough.
4. Be humble. If you don't know the answer to a question, don't be afraid to admit that. As mentioned elsewhere, teams appreciate a

leader who is willing to learn. If we pretend to know everything, we're not in learning mode.
5. Be clear about what you're trying to communicate. Reinforce the key message or messages before you finish the conversation or meeting. Clarity of message is closely related to #2 above – the more we think about what it is we're trying to achieve, the more precise our communications will be.
6. Know your audience. If you are a technologist presenting to a non-technology audience, use plain English. Explain acronyms. Leave time for more questions than you would typically expect. If you're presenting to an executive group, know that their focus is likely to be more on business drivers such as return on investment, more than on the specifics of the solution.
7. Practice. Practice. Practice some more. Every type of verbal communication improves the more we intentionally focus on improving it. Look for coaching if you're uncomfortable doing public speaking. Ask for feedback from staff and peers on how clear you're being. Don't let a meeting finish without confirming with the attendees that they understand your key messages.

Going back to the point I made at the start of this section, in all types of communication, it is essential to remember that what might be clear to you is not necessarily apparent to your audience. If your staff are not all from the same geography, the chances are they will have different first languages and cultural reference points to each other, so it is vital to be as clear and crisp as possible.

Manage your reactions

I was fortunate several years ago to have been nominated, along with a number of my peers, to travel to a company-organised management development course. It was a three-day event held in a ballroom in a large hotel in the US. One of the best things about it was having the opportunity to spend time with and get to know, people in the organisation who I would otherwise not have met.

The content was a mix of things that were new to me and some subjects I was well-versed in. The speakers were a blend of the wonderful and the mediocre, and the team-building exercise had real value – we built bicycles for needy children in that city.

One of the things I took away from the three days was a straightforward, but, I felt, powerful equation:

$$E+R=O$$

(or Event + Response = Outcome)

The formula above resonated with me for a variety of reasons, but let me first explain what it means.

Event: All of us have events in our lives, things that occur every day that we have no control over. A road accident on our commute delays us for 2 hours. An injury requires surgery, causing us to cancel a longed-for holiday. One of our parents becomes ill. We win the Lotto (that last one is obviously on the lower end of probability, but I include it for balance). Events are out of our control.

Response: This is how we react to an event in our day. Do we get angry or upset? Do we overeat? Do we spend too much money? Do we start drinking too much? This part of the equation is the only piece that is within our control. How we react helps determine the outcome.

Outcome: This is the result of the equation. The outcome is only partially within our control, and is influenced, but not dictated, by our Response. If we react positively to an event, with the right mindset and good intent, we can increase the possibility of a positive outcome.

There is a Zen Buddhist fable about a farmer who experiences a series of events. He loses a horse, then gains twelve others. His son breaks his leg. A war breaks out. Due to his injury, the son survives the war, when many others do not. At each stage, the farmer's neighbours say to him "Oh what great/terrible luck". And at after each event, the farmer reacts with "Who can say? We shall see.". He responds with an open mind to each event and doesn't immediately ascribe a positive or negative value to each occurrence.

While I'm not suggesting that it's practical for most of us to adopt this level of equanimity, it is possible to react more positively, and more slowly to events. I've gotten better over the years, but I still have to actively control my responses in the car when another driver behaves rudely or dangerously. If I control my response, I'm less likely to contribute to an increase in bad driving on the road, leading to safer outcomes overall.

The same is true for the rest of our lives. If we're struggling with injury, it's far better to be positive about the outcomes of an unexpected surgery, for example. While it may not change the result, a positive mindset can certainly ease our worries and reduce our stress.

One way to help prepare for unpleasant events is to map out possibilities in our heads, so that if something untoward does occur we have already played out the scenario, and are better able to accept it. I travel roughly every two weeks for my current role, and air travel is notoriously unpredictable. On a recent flight from London to Dublin, we were delayed multiple times (boarding, at the gate, taking off, and then again when we arrived because there was no jet bridge). In total, for a one hour flight, I was delayed by four hours. Unlike some of my fellow passengers, I wasn't particularly upset. I generally accept the fact that delays happen in air travel, and tend to react calmly, and use the time to continue reading, or listening to a podcast or some music. I also consoled myself that I wasn't travelling with small children, which would have made the situation a lot more challenging.

It's not always easy to maintain calm in the face of unplanned events, but it is beneficial, to you and those that you lead. Having a positive or less reactive response to an unexpected event can help drive better outcomes. If we react negatively to a change in circumstances, it can set us back instead of helping to move us forward. If we're managing a team of people and we're handed an un-forecasted budget challenge, we could throw our hands up, and complain about the unfairness of it all. Our team will then follow our lead – that's what teams do – and respond in that fashion themselves. If, instead, we react with "Ok, let's adjust, and move forward." it changes the tone of the conversation and helps us make new plans based on our new reality.

Additionally, by mapping possible outcomes to a situation and having some prepared responses, we reduce the chance of being entirely reactive. Being calm helps others remain calm and lowers the stress levels for you and your team. By managing your reaction to bad news, you help your team in the short term, and also set a positive example for the future.

Manage your hiring

Part of the role of a manager or team lead is to develop a pool of talent for his or her team, and then to foster the development of that talent.

Hiring practices vary significantly from organisation to organisation, and junior and emerging managers often have a limited view as to how those practices drive talent acquisition.

There are a few starting points here:

- Get to know your HR partner. HR often set the rules for hiring, including decision-making around compensation.
- Know the skills you're trying to build in your team.
- Know the culture that you want to build. Hiring someone with the best skills in the world won't help you construct a team culture if that person doesn't share the values you have. Hiring an arrogant so-and-so who feels they are above the rules won't help you build a successful team.
- Develop your network so that you are in a better position to fill vacancies when they arise on your team, either through attrition or growth.
- Develop and document a hiring process so that you can hire consistently and with the necessary speed for your organisation.

I have been through a couple of recessions during my career, and also through boom times. Both sets of market conditions represent challenges for hiring managers.

During boom times, salaries can grow to unsustainable levels. Top talent is highly mobile and can be challenging to attract and retain.

During recessionary times, people can be desperate to get any role that may be on offer. The market can become flooded with qualified candidates, and it can be a challenge to find the best ones for your open position.

These two extremes represent the arc of a pendulum in terms of hiring practices by mid- to large-sized organisations as well. The first type of market favours the candidate and can cause poor behaviours by less mature applicants (failure to show for an interview, accepting roles and not showing up, sandbagging after an offer has been made, etc.). The economically constrained market favours employers, but can lead to poor behaviour on their part – "herding" candidates for group assessments (not treating people as people), pushing starting salaries down for junior entrants, which can have long term impacts, failing to establish good communication practices with candidates, and other dehumanising or unfair practices.

Laszlo Bock's book "Work Rules!" describes the hiring practices and data-driven approaches at Google, when he was head of People Management. It is a fascinating counterpoint to traditional hiring mechanisms and puts hiring the best candidate into a very structured framework. In the early days of Google, the hiring process was fraught with some technically astute but unhelpful questions for assessing candidate suitability – "how many ping-pong balls would fit in a standard school bus?", for example. As Google's hiring process matured, it became more focussed on improving the experience for the candidate, reducing the amount of time required from hiring managers involved, and enhancing the overall outcome – in other words, using data to hire the best person for the role.

Most organisations have a well-intended, if not very efficient hiring process. Large organisations can be especially poor at managing candidate communications, setting expectations and having candidates leave the process feeling like they are valued.

Some suggestions to help you with yours:

- Gather data on the candidates and your process, e.g. how many resumes gathered at different stages in the pipeline, how long a candidate stays in the pipeline, etc.
- With the candidates' permission, retain CVs (if permissible under local data protection laws) even if the candidate wasn't successful. Those in the near-miss category may be suitable for another role in your broader organisation.

- Share information on candidates with other hiring managers, if permitted by HR practices and data protection regulations (e.g. GDPR).
- Hire by committee, rather than having all of the decision-making in the hands of a single hiring manager. Having multiple hiring managers reviewing candidates for a role helps to reduce bias in the hiring process.
- Use questions or tools that allow for a somewhat objective approach to hiring. For example, if hiring software developers, use coding exercises to assess the candidates' ability to think through programming challenges.
- Focus on improving your process every time.

While the steps above won't guarantee you the best candidate for every role, they should improve your outcomes, and hopefully ensure that your hiring process is more pleasant for candidates and more effective for your organisation.

Manage your career

It may seem blindingly obvious, but no-one else is going to manage your career for you. We can build networks, develop sponsors, and put our aspirations in front of senior management, but if those channels don't deliver the opportunities we're looking for, it is up to us to determine what to do about that.

Sometimes we are ambitious but not necessarily skilled. By having the right advisors and mentors, people who will tell us the truth, it is easier to identify when we need to develop a particular set of skills to advance. Sometimes we're not feeling particularly ambitious, and we may be content, due to lower energy levels as mentioned previously, to bide for a while in a role that isn't particularly taxing.

One of the ways to start managing your career is to develop an understanding of what is important to you, and what motivates you. These drivers may change depending on what stage we're at in our development. For example, when I started working, I was far more interested in pure technology roles than I am now. At this point in my career, while I'm interested in how technology can solve business problems, I'm far more interested in strategic roles, and managing teams of people to deliver business outcomes.

I'm also aware of the technical skills that I need to develop to maintain relevance as a technology manager. As part of my learning plan for this year, I'm looking to add another Cloud Service Provider certification, which will help increase the value that I add to my organisation.

It is generally no harm to have a plan to guide your career, so you can identify the roles you wish to transition through to get to your "dream role", should such a thing exist for you. If you're looking to be a Chief

Operating Officer (COO) in 3-5 years, for example, you may want to spend time in a finance role, or a business manager position to develop some of the foundational skills required. It is also beneficial to establish relationships with other COOs in your organisation and outside to get an understanding from them as to what their paths looked like.

The old interview question "Where do you see yourself in five years?" is difficult to answer for most people for a reason. Apart from the inherent difficulties in trying to predict the future, most of us don't have a good view of where we want to be in three years, never mind five. My advice to people working on career planning is to try to identify the roles that will help you build necessary skills to advance to the next "lily pad in the pond", rather than trying to have a comprehensive five-year plan. For example, if my ambition is to become a Chief Technology Officer (CTO) in five or seven years, and I'm a junior developer today, the chances are I will have to advance through a number of roles and spend time as a senior developer, then engineering manager, then group manager before I will have developed the budgetary, technology and people management skills even to be considered for such a role. And in most cases, the path across the pond will not be linear. Charity Majors has written a couple of fascinating articles about the "Engineering Manager pendulum" and the challenges of swinging back and forth between individual contributor and management roles to develop and maintain essential skills. While the articles are specific to technology, the principles may not be.

I mentioned mentors previously. A mentor is someone who will help you identify skill gaps and development opportunities, and will act as an impartial advisor. If you're looking for a mentor in your organisation, it is often best to choose someone who is outside of your immediate management chain. Selecting someone outside of your management hierarchy helps for a couple of reasons. You get a different perspective on the organisation than you would otherwise, and you may feel more confident discussing challenges about your management with someone who is not directly involved.

Getting career advice from HR Learning & Development teams and trusted partners inside and outside your organisation can help you refine your thinking on where you want to go. There are also plenty of books written on the subject. Ram Charan's "The Leadership Pipeline" provides sound advice to anyone looking to understand the changes in behaviour required at different stages or turns in a developing career pipeline, as well as how to build a talent pipeline for an organisation.

Be

Every day we make decisions as to what we are going to focus on; what we are going to do or not do ("there is no try" to quote Yoda). Those choices are what shape the person, and the manager, we will become. This section is all about choosing curiosity, honesty, authenticity, fairness, and other attributes to make yourself a better manager. None of us gets it right every time. By being intentional about who we want to Be, we increase the likelihood of the right outcomes for our staff, our organisations, and ourselves.

Be curious

Life is full of hugely engaging opportunities to learn. It's incredible what we can learn just by asking questions – I believe that asking questions is like an under-used superpower. There are several different mechanisms by which you can constructively leverage curiosity to get to a better or higher-order outcome. The "5 whys" and Fishbone mapping are two related approaches to dig into an issue, for example, to determine the actual root cause.

I recently visited a technology company with my then-boss, where we met with some senior managers at that company. During our meeting, which wasn't under Non-Disclosure Agreement (NDA), I asked some (I thought) incisive questions about their hiring practices, their pipeline and success rates.

As we were walking to my car, my boss said to me "I'm amazed they answered some of the questions you asked." My view, which I shared with him, is that the worst thing that can happen is that the person being questioned declines to answer. If you find yourself running up against a line that causes the other person to start shutting down, pull back to safer territory, and continue with the discussion.

Some thoughts on curiosity:

- Indulge it! If you find something that interests you, and it might be of benefit to you or the organisation or team you serve, pursue it.
- Share what you learn. Hoarding knowledge is so 1980s, as someone told me once. It is empowering to share knowledge, for you and those you with whom you share it. The collective intelligence grows in your organisation if you're generous with your learning.
- Read widely. There are so many incredible insights waiting out there in the world, and so many different areas of study. None of us is likely to live long enough to adequately explore more than a tiny fraction of the world's recorded knowledge.
- Hire for intellectual curiosity. It's a trait that is more relevant and valuable than historical experience unless you are hiring for a very narrow role.
- Look for different sources of ideas. Articles, videos, seminars, even novels and music, any or all of them may offer insights or ideas that can be helpful in trying to solve a problem or trigger a new line of thinking. We're all building on the lessons learned by the generations that went before us.
- Talk to lots of people. I ask questions of taxi drivers, wait staff, people at networking events, my kids' friends' parents. It is interesting how

exploring other people's experiences, and thoughts can lead to insights about the world.
- Be structured in how you leverage your questions (see above on the "5 Whys", for example).
- Don't assume you know the answer to something unless you're a recognised subject-matter expert (and even then, proceed with caution). Ray Dalio refers to this as being radically open-minded.

In short, don't underestimate the power of curiosity and use it to feed your development.

Be available

"My door is always open" is such a management cliché – one that we've all heard many times. It is also clearly a lie. The idea that any manager in a busy organisation can have random, unscheduled drop-ins at any point of the day or week is not a sustainable one.

Several approaches can be put in place to ensure that when your staff need you, that you can be available to them. Some possibilities:

- Team meetings – although it may not always be suitable for people to raise issues (particularly personal ones), depending on the culture of the organisation. In software engineering organisations, scrum meetings or daily stand-up calls are not unusual but are focused on practical deliverables.

- Clinic hours – set times in your calendar every week where people know that they can drop-in if required to discuss an unscheduled issue.
- Regularly scheduled one-to-one meetings. These can be daily, weekly, monthly or even quarterly, depending on the individual requirement and the closeness of the functional relationship.
- Ad hoc conversations – sometimes someone will stop you in the corridor or canteen with a request or discussion item. In some cases, based on the topic, it may be appropriate to deal with it there and then; in others, it may be best to schedule a time to discuss in private.

When we have time with our staff, it is essential that we're present with them, and actively listening. If we can't concentrate because the time isn't right, it is better (and kinder) to schedule a follow-up meeting to discuss the issue properly.

Being available isn't just about being physically and mentally present. It also involves being emotionally available, a phrase that smacks of pop-psychology at its worst. What I mean by it in this context is that it is crucial to connect with the people we work with at a human level. We need to demonstrate vulnerability to build trust – sharing our failures and failings, being willing to share our thoughts, discussing our families. We are all human, and we all struggle at different points in our lives. Being emotionally available allows our staff to share their concerns in a safe environment. Of course, as with any relationship, it takes time to build up a level of trust and allow for genuine exchanges. It is also the case that different people are more or less comfortable with varying degrees of openness or vulnerability in the workplace. With each team and individual, we learn where those lines are through experience.

Be emotionally intelligent

I first came across decently written information on EQ (Emotional Quotient, aka Emotional Intelligence) reading Jo Owen's books in the early 2000s. As a more logical thinker, I wasn't sure of the value of bringing emotion to the workplace. What I failed to recognise then, and have since learned, is that emotion is unavoidable. Rationally-made decisions would seem to be best, but the truth is that emotion plays a part in all the choices we make. It has been discovered that people who sustain damage to their amygdala (which plays a central role in emotion) can become blocked when it comes to decision-making (PubMed article). They can become totally indecisive, which appears contrary to a more logical-leaning view of how we make decisions.

We react emotionally much faster than we can think. There have been many books written about how we share our brains with an emotional being who can take the controls more quickly than our "thinking" self can react.

While we have speedy emotional reactions, it is possible to identify those physical responses that indicate that we are in an emotionally reactive state. We can feel our shoulders come up when we're tense. Our voice may become higher-pitched, and we may speak more loudly. We may feel ourselves becoming literally hot under the collar, as stress hormones kick in. In a situation where we've become angry, we may even bunch our fists, as if getting ready to fight physically.

When we become experienced at first of all recognising those physical responses and second of all, the triggers that cause them, it can give us time to respond in a more thoughtful, less reactive way.

It helps to take a pause and breathe. Taking a quick breather can give us the time required to understand why we're reacting emotionally instead of logically to a situation.

Ray Dalio refers to the concept of the higher- and lower-level selves, where the lower-level identity is the emotionally-driven self, primarily based in the amygdala, and the higher-level identity is the cortically-based conscious awareness.

We need to understand when we're reacting because of our emotions, and when we are thinking logically. This understanding is important from both a personal interaction perspective and also when we are trying to make informed intelligent decisions.

Practice recognising your emotional state, particularly when it leads you to have unhelpful interactions or make bad decisions (sometimes the two are linked). Identify the triggers to your emotional responses:

- Is someone questioning you in a way you don't like? Is your ego getting in the way?
- Are you reacting to the tone someone has used rather than the content? Separate the message from the messenger.
- Are you responding to something which has happened in the past? Did you have a bad commute, and you're still frustrated because you were late? Did you have a row with your partner or spouse, and you're carrying that into the workplace?

Taking time to identify and acknowledge the emotional responses we have and making sure that they are not negatively impacting our work interactions and decision-making is a crucial skill, and it takes time to develop. In my opinion, it is one well worth investing in.

Be vulnerable

It can be tough early in our careers (and sometimes later as well) to admit that we don't know everything, particularly when we are supposed to be "in charge".

When I was starting what has become my career, it was incredibly rare to hear any leader admit to failings or flaws. The gulf between them and me was vast – there was no connection, and as a result, no real relationship.

I looked up to some of the senior managers I knew early in my career, but they were very much unknown quantities, and I didn't fully trust them as a result.

People respond to vulnerability by sharing their own. In "The Culture Code: The Secrets of Highly Successful Groups", Daniel Coyle writes that the sharing of vulnerability between members of a group is critical to building trust. Leaders or managers who profess to know everything set themselves up for failure, and close off critical dialogue. Coyle provides some compelling examples of where the willingness of a leader or manager to admit that they didn't have all the answers led to much better outcomes than could otherwise be expected. There's a particularly good example in Chapter 7 of that book where he describes the interactions between the captain of a plane that has suffered catastrophic control failures and the crew. I won't reproduce it here, but I recommend you read the book – it covers the topic particularly well.

When you are working with your team, it is vital to be willing to admit that you don't have all the answers and to ask your team for their input. Just as important is to then act on that input, so team members can see that you are taking them seriously.

Not only is this important for team cohesion and function, but it is also favourable for morale. People who feel that they can influence the direction of something also feel a sense of ownership and pride when it works out. If we're just "following orders" we don't have that sense of connection to the outcomes.

Another central element of being vulnerable is admitting when you're wrong. Again, this is a tough habit to build, but it is imperative to building trust. It also sets the tone for your team and how team members will behave with each other and with other groups. We are all wrong many times during the day and week. We make assumptions and act on incomplete information. We let our biases direct us without questioning them thoroughly. It is essential to admit when we are wrong as soon as we become aware, preferably in front of the team. It doesn't have to be a hand-wringing mea culpa – just a simple admission that being human, we have screwed up, and will try to do better in future.

One of the best ways to demonstrate vulnerability, and a willingness to learn is to ask detailed, thoughtful questions.

I've described asking questions elsewhere as a kind of neglected superpower. We can learn so much just by asking simple questions. Subject matter experts will gladly distil knowledge into digestible answers if they think you are asking humbly and in good faith – saving you the time required to learn something from scratch. Members of your team will share details of their lives with you and help you build a connection with them if you ask genuinely, and listen to the answers.

I struggle with remembering names and faces (my wife jokes that if I didn't see her at least once a week, I wouldn't know who she is) , but by asking questions of my teams about their lives and family every time we have one-to-one meetings I learn more about them and share things about my own family with them. This kind of sharing brings us closer together, and I believe, helps make us more effective as a team. It also helps me exercise the mental muscles required to retain personal information – something at which I don't naturally excel.

Asking questions can also surprise people into revealing things that they wouldn't otherwise – things that might prove helpful in building team cohesion or addressing underlying tensions that you might not be aware of.

Be willing to be vulnerable. None of us knows everything, and by admitting that we make ourselves more human and relatable to our staff.

Be a networker

What do we mean when we talk about networking? For me, it's making connections – becoming a nexus point in an organisation or community. Introducing yourself to as many people as possible, because you never know when that connection may be helpful to yourself or someone else. When I'm talking with mentoring groups and junior managers about networking, I always use the analogy of building bridges – it's a lot easier to do when you're not under pressure than when you're "under fire."

In the book, "Tribal Networking", Dave Logan and his co-authors write about forming triads, or three-pointed relationships, as being the desirable state of a network for individuals and managers aiming to improve their culture. Most people, when they start networking, focus more on "dyadic" or two-party groupings, which puts the person making the connection in the middle of everything. These types of structures are not scalable, and ultimately deliver far less value than those based on multi-point connections. Bringing two people together with shared interests and capabilities, and then removing yourself from the conversation, amplifies the networking effect. It also returns value to you personally, because both parties will appreciate you connecting them. If you do this regularly, you will develop a reputation as someone who bridges parts of the organisation and its partners together.

The great thing about networking broadly in an organisation is that you learn a tremendous amount. It is astounding to me how few people understand the value of networking, especially early in their careers.

On the other hand, networking can be challenging, especially if you are on the introverted end of the spectrum, but it is well worth the effort. A key thing when meeting someone new for the first time is to try and make a connection. Asking people about themselves and their interests will usually spark a good conversation – we all like to talk about ourselves. Look for ways to maintain your network as you go – check-ins with vital people in your network should be reasonably regular (a few times a year, on an agreed schedule).

It took me a long time to become comfortable with networking at events, and I still find it challenging. I find it a lot easier to make one-to-one approaches now than I did early in my career. Whenever I travel to a new office, I will doorstop people and ask them about themselves and their role. I then look for ways to add value, by introducing my new contact to others, or suggesting some reading material, or volunteering to assist with a project or problem they have (again, depending on the individual).

Networking well increases your value to the organisation you work in, and to yourself. It allows you to see more broadly than your natural organisational boundary (team, group, division, etc.) and will allow you to add value to others in your network.

I strongly recommend that everyone who works for me spend a portion of their week on building and maintaining networks. As mentioned, introverts can find it awkward and uncomfortable, but if we do it well, the rewards are substantial, and it becomes more comfortable with practice.

Be politically aware

Jo Owen, in his book "How to Manage" lays out the importance of Political Quotient, or PQ, by labelling the entire section – "PQ skills– making things happen".

I have often heard individual contributors and junior managers refer disparagingly to internal politics as being something they refuse to engage in.

This position is a very naïve one, in my opinion, and it comes from a place where people have not had to navigate large organisations or develop cross-functional relationships to get things done.

There are centres of political power in every organisation, and knowing who they are and what they are responsible for can be critical to success.

Every group of people becomes political over time. Even those that start from a place of shared intent and mission can split into factions quite quickly. The story of how the Women's March movement in the US divided along racial and religious lines is an illuminating reminder of how easy it is for groups of people to divide ourselves into "us" and "them".

Jo Owen writes about how political skills may seem Machiavellian, but they are necessary. In his view, people who are intelligent (high IQ) and have excellent interpersonal skills (high EQ) will often be confined to backwaters in the organisation if they don't have sufficiently developed PQ skills.

In essence, PQ skills involve the obtaining and leveraging of power in an organisation to get things done. While this may seem distasteful to some, this is how successful individuals can deliver. The sources of political clout that Mr Owen writes about are:

1. Money
2. Information
3. Skills
4. Customers
5. Access
6. Permissions
7. Scarce resource

I'm not going to go through these in detail, although I do recommend his book to all budding managers. Some of the items on the above list are relatively self-explanatory, but I will dig into #5 a little – Access.

Every senior decision-maker has a gatekeeper – usually an Executive Assistant, but it can be a COO, depending on the type of access required.

It is vitally important to know who the decision-makers are with the ability to impact your success; either through providing sponsorship, providing or withholding budget, or making final calls on hiring or other critical decisions. It is then essential to develop relationships with them and their gatekeepers. While this may seem somewhat manipulative, being kind (detailed below) is a genuine way to have positive relationships with often undervalued, usually overworked gatekeepers.

By developing strong working relationships with gatekeepers, you increase your ability to access the decision-makers when you need them. In other words, build bridges before you need them, so when you're in trouble that access is available to you.

Be honest

Honesty may seem to some to be a strange trait to focus on in a book about management, but it is fundamental to building trust. We all need trust to be successful.

What do I mean by honesty in the context of the workplace?

- Own your mistakes. If you screw up, put your hand up and admit it immediately. I've mentioned this elsewhere as being necessary for building healthy team dynamics.
- Don't take responsibility for other's successes – celebrate your team's success instead.

- Be clear with your staff and your peers about areas of improvement. If you're honest with them, there's a better chance they'll help you see your blind-spots and focus areas.
- Live your values. For example, if you talk about an inclusive workplace, don't stand by while someone is made to feel uncomfortable for who they are, or what they believe.
- Don't stab people in the back or gossip about others. If you wouldn't say it to their face with good intent, don't say it.

There's not a lot more to this, in my opinion. Let people know where you stand, then be consistent in that. It ties into the next topic, authenticity, and it also aligns very closely to demonstrating integrity in the workplace and outside.

Be authentic

When I started working first, bosses remained aloof, and the command and control approach to management was the norm. We were told how high to jump and what shoes to wear while doing it. In the early days of my management career, I adopted a somewhat similar style because that was what I had experienced, and what I thought was required to be a good manager. Through reading, building (sometimes painful) experience, and spending time to understand my personal style and motivation, I discovered that this was not the best way to manage.

I'm not a dictatorial individual. I prefer to work on a collaborative basis with my team members and peers and to find ways to engage people. Being prescriptive and command-focussed didn't seem natural to me – it was inauthentic to who I am. Fortunately, I learned this relatively early in my career, and shifted to a more inclusive style of management, focussed on understanding how to get the best out of people.

Being authentic is closely related to being honest, in my opinion. If you're not putting on a mask or a front, and you're not trying to be anyone other than yourself, it's very liberating. It's also a lot less tiring than trying to manufacture a work persona that you have to maintain on an ongoing basis.

Being authentic also means standing up for your values. If you believe that something is wrong, you have to be willing to say that. It means "telling the truth to power" if required; for example, if your boss is behaving in a way that is not helpful to the organisation, you have to be willing to tell them that constructively.
Conversations of this kind can be hugely uncomfortable, and may not go your way in the short term. That said, if you sit by and let your manager fail, you are culpable in that failure if you didn't try to help them.

If someone does something in your eyesight or earshot that you know contravenes the values of the organisation, you have to be willing to stand against that. Failure to do so will result in conflict within yourself. You may find that the conflict becomes so strong that you feel the need to leave the organisation in extreme cases. Again, the important thing is to behave consistently and authentically in a way which mirrors your values. That doesn't mean that we don't use work-appropriate language in the workplace or leave contentious subjects (e.g. politics, religion) out of workplace discussions, but it does mean being true to ourselves.

People are generally pretty good at subconsciously identifying other people who are inauthentic, and while they may not consciously identify why, they won't trust those individuals. Trust, shared values and a "noble cause" are required attributes for organisations to evolve, according to David Logan in "Tribal Leadership".

Be organised

I have met and worked with some "super-organised" people in the course of my career. Goal-driven individuals who make personally-owned multi-year plans and execute against them with rigour. I recently worked with a mentee who told me she had completed her 3-year development program in just 2 – which I found both personally embarrassing and slightly horrifying. Most of us are not like this. We can procrastinate, or fail to prioritise. In the section titled "Manage your time." I mentioned approaches that work for time planning, but being organised is more than this.

We all have different approaches to manage our day. Some people wing it as they go; others are incredibly task-focussed and drive their lives through lists. How people choose to organise themselves may, in part, be a consequence of personality or thinking styles as referenced in Section 1.

When I started working, I leant more towards the "winging it" end of the spectrum. As I've gotten older, and hopefully more experienced, I've discovered that I can't manage the conflicting demands of my day without some variant of a plan.

These days I typically organise myself from a day-to-day perspective using task lists in whatever the corporate tool of choice is (Outlook, at the time of writing). I find having time-bounded task lists with the ability to prioritise makes it much less likely that I will drop something. I have a lot of context-switching in my current roles, and without some form of structured tracking, I would very likely lose sight of work.

I also have a structure for files on my laptop, which, while not entirely consistent, at least allows me to find things with a minimum of fuss.

For example, for notes from a meeting or speaking notes, I use plain Windows Notepad files. These work well for me for a few reasons:

1. They are tiny from a disk space perspective – the notes I take from a multi-hour meeting will

typically amount to less than 80KB in disk storage.
2. Portability – plain text files can be read on any device, and will still very likely be readable on any device in the future.
3. Searchability – Windows can index plain text files which makes it easier to find specific content.

I use a consistent naming structure for these notes so that I can easily find them. With meeting notes, I use the structure mtg_notes_<meeting_name>_DDMMYYYY. For long-running meeting series, this allows me to easily find and group the related minutes, even a couple of years later.

Within the text files for a meeting, when I'm taking notes, I use an asterisk (*) to denote an action, and I write the name of the assignee and expected date of completion next to it. When I'm sending the notes out to attendees after the meeting, it is usually pretty trivial for me to then copy and paste the text of the minutes into an email.

I'm not suggesting that this approach will work for everyone, but I've tried many other methods that aren't as "low tech", and they didn't work. I tried a Lightscribe pen at one point, and thought it was the business – I was able to take notes in a proprietary notepad and then upload the notes automatically to my computer. I was also able to record audio during meetings –

something that became much more problematic once privacy concerns came more to the fore. In the end, I had to give up the pen, because the ink cartridges had an impractically small amount of ink in each one, and it was only possible to record notes using the specially printed notebooks, which became prohibitively expensive.

On the lower-tech end of the spectrum, I had boxes of A4 notebooks from multiple jobs in my attic at one point, which was completely hopeless. There is no way to search or digitise these notes quickly, and no point in having the notebooks after a year or so. While I like to write in a notebook when I'm in a one-to-one or one-to-small number meeting, I always use my laptop to take notes when I'm in a more substantial gathering, being careful not to let it distract me too much. If I do use paper-based records, I transcribe them into a Notepad file on my computer as soon as is practical, so I don't lose the actions or content of the meeting.

Since we're on the subject of meetings, I always try to send out agenda items in advance and meeting notes within 24 hours so that people can review the assigned actions. This behaviour ties closely to "Being considerate of others' time.". Don't have people chase you for information that you should have provided without prompting.

My recommendation is to find a method that works for you and apply it consistently. At this stage in my career,

I consider it to be vaguely worrying when I speak with a team member, and they don't have a consistent mechanism to organise themselves and their activities.

Be a team player

Teams are the building blocks of every organisation in which I've worked. In a large organisation, there are many teams which make up departments, groups, lines of business and divisions.

Being a team player does not just mean supporting your immediate team. It means supporting the goals of the entire organisation to make sure we are collectively successful in delivering for our customers.

If we become too focussed on our immediate team, we may lose sight of the fact that other teams in the organisation are all working towards the same goals.

Patrick Lencioni, in his book "The Five Dysfunctions of a Team", introduces the concept of the "first team" – in this case, the executive team you may be a part of when you graduate to being a senior manager in your organisation. This book offers terrific insights into how top-level management teams can misfire because of a lack of trust or alignment. The same is true in my experience of teams at all levels in an organisation.

We need to be aware of the organisation goals and how the work our teams do connects to those goals. We have to be willing to work hard for the team to ensure that we're carrying our share of the burden. Being a team player in the context of our local team is ensuring that we're covering our peers – for example, if there's an on-call rotation in place for a support organisation, team players will hold each other accountable for ensuring that the rotations for support are fairly distributed.

Being a team player in a broader context means saying "Yes" to things more. Yes, to sharing resources; Yes, to providing support to someone who is struggling; Yes, to doing more to build the team ethos and delivering on the organisational goals.

Stanley McChrystal, in his book "Team of Teams" gives some great examples of how this worked in practice when he pulled together a diverse structure of Special Operations (Spec Ops) groups when he was Commander of Joint Special Operations Command (JSOC) in Afghanistan. It's a great read on how to make a single functional team out of many diverse, distrusting and siloed teams. Spec Ops teams focus heavily on team culture, which is built up over time through gruelling training and extremely tough exercises and missions. The differing cultures within the teams often lead to rivalry and distrust between, e.g. Seal Teams and Delta Force, or Delta and Army Rangers. The lack of trust is not primarily because there is a lack of respect between the forces at a broad level – it is more because the intimate, highly-functional team culture creates a harder line than most between "us" and "them". Members of established Spec Ops groups have been through hell together and trust each other to a higher degree than usual as a result. They frequently refer to each other as brothers or family.

Corporate cultures are very rarely this tight even at the small team level, except in the case of some high-performing organisational cultures. That said, the siloes that exist in larger organisations can lead to similar challenges between teams; lack of trust and respect leads to a failure to see the bigger picture – that all units serve the end goals of the broader organisation, usually to provide service to a customer.

Stanley McChrystal explains how he built a team culture that many organisations would be extremely envious of, from a starting position of limited trust and almost no sharing. By the mid-point of his tenure in Afghanistan, teams that would typically not exchange the time of day were sharing critical, short-supply resources like helicopters for the good of the overall mission. Instead of being focussed on what their immediate team needed, they were thinking and acting broadly in support of the entire mission, in a "team of teams" construct.

Being a team player means knowing the goals of your immediate team, your partner teams and the overall organisation, and doing what is within your power to advance those goals. Not always an easy task, but one that all of us should be willing to answer.

Be a customer advocate

When we work in small to mid-size companies, we're often quite close to the end customer and may interact with them directly. We develop and support products that are directly linked to revenue and customer satisfaction. As organisations become larger, it is more common to work in parts of the company that never have direct interactions with customers.

I've worked in technology teams and groups for my entire career. In my current role, I work in a large organisation in which technical teams never get to meet real end-customers. This situation is a missed opportunity, in my opinion. Understanding the needs of the customers who drive the business helps all of us know how our contributions help those customers. By supporting the customer, we're doing the right thing, and hopefully seeing growth in the company as a result. Companies generally only exist to serve some customer need, or they don't survive. Derek Sivers, in his book "Anything you want: 40 lessons for a new kind of entrepreneur", writes compellingly of serving the customer. When he ran his business, customer service was all that mattered to him. In his case, his customers were musicians and the people who wanted to listen to their music, and he filtered all of his decision-making through the lens of their requirements. He could have made a lot more money in the short term going in a different direction, but that didn't align with his values or the reason that he set up his company.

Other companies take this customer-centric view to what could be considered extremes. Amazon has as one of its core values being customer-obsessed and hires people who behave in this way. Companies like Zappos Shoes (now an Amazon company) also put the customer first, and advocate strongly for them. In one company blog post, Zappos describe themselves as "maniacally obsessed" with customer service.

If we're working directly with customers, it is easier to be an advocate for them. We can understand them as people, and help clarify their needs. We can then act on their behalf in our groups and organisations.

When we're further away from the front line, we need to identify our internal stakeholders, who are a proxy for the customer that the company delivers service to. In other words, we have to advocate for our stakeholders and make sure they get what they need to serve their customers. This advocacy then becomes a virtuous chain that impacts the end-customer outcomes.

If you are part of a decision-making group and you feel that something is going to go against the needs of your core customers, speak up. Make the customer's voice heard. Make it clear that your group exists to deliver for your customer. I believe that if enough people in companies did that we wouldn't be dealing with many situations like Enron, the Libor scandals, or a large number of other corporate misdeeds and ethics violations.

Be considerate of others' time

How many times have you hosted or shown up to a meeting and it doesn't start on time because attendees are late? How often have those individuals sent a note in advance to say they'll be delayed and to start without them?

Everyone has a lot to do during a working day. Everyone is entitled to the fundamental respect and professional courtesy that all of us would like to have from our co-workers.

If you're responsible for scheduling a meeting, consult attendees' calendars first. Consider the time zones your attendees are based in and plan accordingly. I've worked in the EMEA region for most of my career, and there have been countless meetings scheduled during that time by US colleagues at extremely family-unfriendly times. If you work in the US and your team members are in India, take into account where they are based and do your best to find times that work for everyone. Also, if there's a regular series of meetings and one time-zone is always going to be disadvantaged, make it a rotation. In other words, if India suffers through late attendance one week, the equitable thing to do is to have US staff attend an early meeting the following week.

If you work in an organisation that is addicted to meetings, the chances are that meetings will start on the hour and half-hour mark. Consider scheduling the start time of your session at 5 minutes past the hour or half-hour, and finish early if possible. That will give your attendees time to transit between meetings, or take a quick "comfort break". Again, we've all had lots of days in our careers where meetings are back-to-back, and it becomes challenging merely to be on time, never mind deal with anything else. Take that into account when you plan for others.

If you're an attendee and know you're not going to make a meeting, notify the organiser. If you are not critical, they have the option to proceed without you. If you are a vital contributor to the meeting, make sure to work with them on rescheduling. If you're going to be late, let the organiser know that too. If you are a presenter, don't be late – if possible, set up material in advance, and have any technology (phones, video conference, Telepresence, etc.) established before the call and tested.

These things all seem pretty obvious, but it's incredible how few people demonstrate basic meeting etiquette when it comes to scheduling and responding to others' meetings.

Finally, on the subject of meeting etiquette, don't hog the floor. If you have a point to make, do it quickly, and don't grandstand – that's also being respectful of others' time.

Be a continuous learner

We are all supposed to be continuous learners in the modern age. Many studies show that the brain is incredibly plastic, and we can continue to acquire new skills right up until we die. In fact, it has been discovered that learning actively on an ongoing basis is a great way to prevent your brain from atrophying. Research papers from the Karolinska Institute in Sweden* and others show an 11% reduction in the risk of Alzheimer's Disease for every additional year of education.

Does this mean that we need to stay in formal education indefinitely? Not at all – it means that we need to look to develop new skills and learning pathways continuously.

I refer to this "intentional learning". We all learn continuously anyway – whether it is through accident or design. From the trivial – learning the shortest journey to work at certain times of the day to the more meaningful – learning how to communicate more effectively with teenage children – we all develop throughout our lives.

We need a plan, though, if we're to make the most of the time we have. Typically, at the mid-point in our lives, we are pretty time-poor. Working parents with children are often exhausted and can be very time-constrained indeed. For those of us in this category, it is more important than ever to develop an intentional approach to maximising learning time.

We, therefore, need to understand:

- What our learning goals are. What do we want to achieve through this learning? By when?
- What our preferred style of learning is – hands-on, reading, classroom-based, etc.
- When we learn best – what time of day are we most receptive?
- How we can reinforce what we learn – new knowledge can often fall into the "use it or lose it" category as far as our brains are concerned.

By developing an annual learning plan, and updating it as we progress, we can both track our progress and adjust our approaches as necessary. And as managers, we set an example for our teams to follow – if we prioritise learning, so will our staff.

Be kind

One of my first jobs out of college was on the University campus that I had just graduated from. I worked in a group that was part of the Computer Science department, and we were doing things that were cutting edge at the time. The smarter members of the group were involved in video transmission technology, and I was building one of the very first college websites. I also developed one of the first "clickable" maps of Ireland using then-revolutionary "imagemap" technology. When I think about how far the Web has come from the days post-Gopher, I realise how old I am.

My boss at the time was a highly intelligent but challenging individual. He didn't have a lot of time for lesser intellects than his, and I was not the smartest member of the team. I was on the receiving end of a lot of shouted verbal abuse as a result. He often made me feel very small. I realise now that he struggled with human interaction generally, but at the time, given my lack of maturity, it felt very personal. Several years later, his company ended up contracting to the company I moved to. In essence, he ended up reporting to me.

I could have made some hay from the change in circumstances, but I was aware enough at the time to realise why that would be a bad idea. We often hear – "be kind on the way up because you don't know who you will meet on the way down." While the circumstances certainly changed the power dynamic, I don't think that's a great motivation – Karmic resonance aside – for being kind to people.

I think it's more important to be kind because it helps to get the best out of people. If we focus on doing the right thing for someone else, we will naturally be kind. And by being kind, I don't mean sugar-coating hard truths – it is more helpful to be honest with someone than to help them hide from their failings. We all need assistance in recognising where we need to improve, and it is a kindness to take the time to help someone develop. To be clear, being kind doesn't mean "being nice". It can be necessary to tell hard truths bluntly. Being *nice* doesn't help anyone develop, nor does it help you get things done.

Kindness means treating people with dignity and respect. Everyone is a person, with their baggage, their challenges and their hopes and aspirations. It is not our place to squash someone else's dreams or to diminish their potential. Our job as managers and leaders is to do the opposite – to make the workplace a safe place for people to try and fail, and try again. By doing so, we also set a new generation of managers on a path where they will be kind and will foster a culture of development and inclusivity in their teams.

Be reasonably unreasonable

I think of myself as a reasonable person. I like people to feel comfortable, and I tend to be careful about how I couch criticism and advice as a result. I have been told that can sometimes dilute the message. As a result, I'm working on being more direct without being hurtful. (According to Daniel Coyle, in his book "The Culture Code", the "sandwich approach" to giving critical feedback sandwiched between positive feedback doesn't work – on the contrary, it can confuse people. Give one message at a time.)

Extremely unreasonable people are hard to work with. That said, people who are unreasonable for *a good reason* are often those who change the world. I have written about such people in an article at my blog site (www.amusingmulcahy.com) and provided a counterpoint to that approach.

Being too reasonable (or too unreasonable) can be a recipe for disaster, or at least for a lack of progress. Being "reasonably unreasonable" means not accepting the status quo. Steve Jobs was unreasonable. Bill and Melinda Gates, through their foundation, are unyielding about what they're trying to change – but by being so, they are changing the world.

How does this play out in practice? It means not accepting the first answer given to you. Asking second-order questions, and focussing on the core of issues, helps develop your team. Pushing people to take on roles they may not feel they are ready for helps them develop; in my own experience, I've never grown faster than when I've felt distinctly uncomfortable. Not accepting the first design, or the first deliverable, without adequate discussion, debate and scrutiny. There are many stories of people who worked for apparently unreasonable individuals only to later realise that they were being pushed to improve by their boss.

Working for someone who continuously tells you you're doing a great job doesn't help you develop. By contrast, working for someone who challenges you, pushes you, and is generally unreasonable in a positive way, can help you develop rapidly. Being comfortable at times isn't a bad thing, but constant comfort makes us soft. We lose our edge. When you manage a team, while you want people to belong, and feel they are part of the team and the organisation, you also need to know when to push, and when to be unreasonable.

Be resilient

Every life is a mixture of rain and sun. We all encounter difficulty in our lives and those who are resilient use that adversity to grow and become better. The old saying "What doesn't kill me makes me stronger" is only partially true, but it is my experience that having to struggle strengthens us.

Just so we're clear, when I think about resiliency, I am referring to the ability to "bounce back" from difficulties or unexpected events or to deal with stressors. Systemic resiliency, like that built into cloud-scale platforms like Netflix, is the resiliency to survive multiple component failures and still deliver service. Most humans are capable of being resilient (although we're not necessarily designed to deal with numerous systemic failures and bounce back). There is also the implication that resiliency implies learning from unexpected events, to be stronger in the future, and the sense that resilient people tend to persevere through adversity. Angela Duckworth writes about this in her book "Grit", and speaks about it in Ted talks.

I attended a talk recently by a performance coach who made a fascinating point. He talked about the stress response curve, which is the inverted "U-curve" shown below, which was originated by PG Nixon.

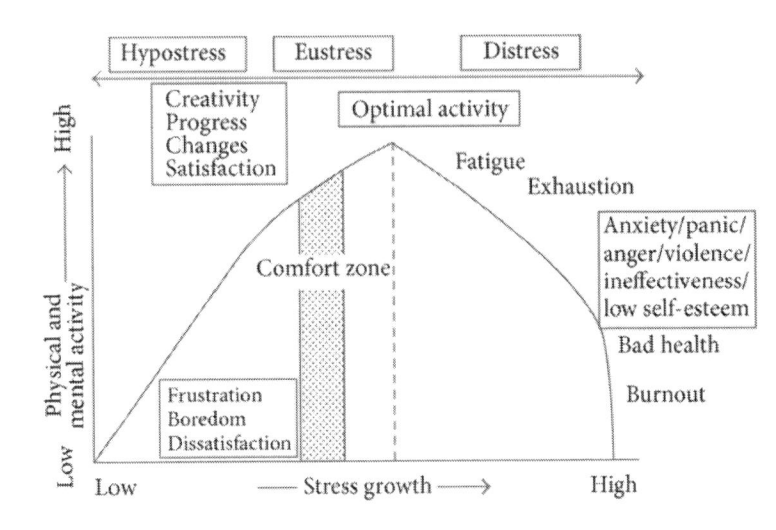

Image Licensed under Creative Commons: Source www.researchgate.net

We are often told that stress is bad for us. The reality is that too much, or too little pressure is damaging for us, but there is an optimal level of stress in our lives that enables us to be productive.

Too much stress and we burn out. Too little, and boredom sets in, which can lead to another form of burnout and a sort of cognitive decline over time.

When we're in an over-stressed mode, it is essential to be resilient and to aim to reduce the impact of that stress on ourselves. On the other hand, it can be beneficial to introduce pressure to drive optimal performance, but the line between that and the adverse effects of stress overload is not very wide.

The amount of time we're under stress is also critical. Short term, acute stress, can be an impetus, as shown above. Long-term (or chronic) stress can lead to significant adverse impacts on physiology and on behaviour. Overeating, reliance on alcohol or medications, and other undesirable responses can all be symptoms of a chronic stress response.

The most important thing, as quoted by the performance coach and by many other sources, is the approach we take to view stress.

- Do we adopt a positive mental approach to stressful situations?
- Do we manage our sleep, exercise, diet and other physical needs well?
- If chronic stress continues, do we seek to reduce it through changing jobs, or removing other sources of stress?

I've mentioned E+R=O in the section on managing your response to events, in the hope of improving the outcome. This approach to stress events can help to build resilience and drive momentum.

Building a resilient mindset helps us to remain calm under stressful conditions. By maintaining our composure, we are better able to make the best possible decisions and to lead others. While some people are naturally inclined to keep cool in the face of adversity, most of us have to work at it. Being able to flex with the shocks that life throws our way will help us weather those shocks. In high winds, trees are often able to bend, but not break – that should be our approach as well.

Be consistent

Consistency is an essential trait for managers (as much as for parents). Inconsistency makes people feel unsure, and by making them uncertain, we make them unsafe. Consistency in approach is far easier to maintain if you are authentic, as called out in an earlier section.

What does consistency mean in practice? That someone behaves in the same way regardless of the person with whom they are interacting. I recently had a conversation with a colleague who was expressing concern that, because of his apparent youthfulness, and his enthusiasm for his subject matter, he wouldn't be taken seriously by his stakeholders. He thought that these factors might be holding him back from senior roles. He wanted my advice on how to have more gravitas, but he didn't want to alter how he presented himself. To me, this observation was a smart one on his part – by deciding to be authentically himself, he would not have to maintain the mental energy to put up a "senior management façade". My advice to him was to slow down his speaking pace. He is a highly intelligent, very well-read and educated individual, and because of his knowledge in specific areas is a known, trusted advisor to senior leaders. All he needs to do to cement that is to be himself, just at a slightly slower pace. By slowing down his speech, it will also give him time to think more in between speaking. In addition, slowing down speech can lower our voice, which adds to gravitas or presence.

Another individual who comes to mind, a senior leader, is **exactly** the same whether he is talking with a junior colleague in a corridor, meeting with a regulator or presenting to a group of other senior leaders on a strategic topic. He is known, and respected, for being entirely consistent in his representation of himself.

In the management of teams, consistency means holding everyone to the same standards. By failing to do this, we can create the appearance of favouritism. Even the perception of "playing favourites" can be toxic to team culture and can undermine your ability to manage the group. If someone makes a mistake, help them learn from it. If the error is visible at a senior level, take ownership of it – after all, you're running the team. Jocko Willink and Leif Babin cover this extensively in their book "Extreme Ownership". If there are challenges in interactions between individuals, develop a consistent approach for dealing with them.

Make the rules and values of the team explicit, and then apply them consistently. Reward people for behaving in a way that is coherent with the team or organisation values, and correct, firmly but fairly, those instances where people miss the mark.

Deliver according to the expectations you've set for yourself and the team. If you agree on a set of dates with a stakeholder for deliverables, meet or beat those targets. If for reasons beyond your control you are unable to, reset the expectations in plenty of time, and apologise for the miss (even if it wasn't your fault directly).

Again, by being consistent, you build trust with your team, partners and senior stakeholders. High-performing cultures are consistently seen to be high in both trust and safety, and consistency in management helps to build both.

Be action-oriented
During the period that I was writing this book, I wrote a blog post (https://www.amusingmulcahy.com/?p=430) on the Marine Corps' evaluation system for

performance management. You would quite correctly assume that the US Marines are an action-oriented group. I found out about that evaluation system through listening to one of Jocko Willink's podcasts. Jocko is an ex-Navy Seal and is probably the face that stares back at you if you look up "action-oriented" in a dictionary. One of his favourite phrases is "Get After It". Jocko's philosophy of life is concisely summed up in "Discipline – A Field Manual", which is brutally simple in its direction – stop making excuses, and go get stuff done. Or in Jocko's words:

"Where do you start? You start right **HERE**. When do you start? You start right **NOW**. You initiate action. You **GO**."

I bring up Jocko and that podcast (#174, if you are interested) because there was one quote in it (among many others) that strongly resonated with me:

"You can't think things better."

While this seems simplistic on the surface, we can all get stuck in the habit of thinking too much and not doing enough. There are a couple of terms that relate to this - "analysis paralysis" or searching for a perfect data picture before making a decision and moving forward.

Thinking is obviously necessary – it helps us understand the world around us, and helps us craft a direction to move forward in. I'm not advocating action without thought, but I agree with the quote. Thinking by itself doesn't change anything in the world outside of our heads.

Avoiding analysis paralysis and not mistaking procrastination for preparation is vital to making things happen. The Marine Corps definition describes **Initiative** as *driving actions from opportunity* – being proactive. We need to do what we can with what we have **now**. We will never have all the information we think we need or all the funding we feel we need or all the time we think we need. All we have is what we have now, this minute. So, we start on what needs to be done, and we make progress.

As an aside, on the subject of having additional information before starting, there was an interesting study done which showed that giving professional gamblers more information made them less successful. When the players in the study were only given five pieces of information about horses in an upcoming race, they were more successful in identifying winners than on being given twenty pieces of information. Ironically, the more information they got, and the less successful they became, the more confident they grew in their predictions about winners. Another lesson to take from the quote above then is that additional information can not only delay us, but it can also make us more confident in making the wrong decisions.

Look for opportunities to take action to make a difference, and take those opportunities. Demonstrating initiative (in getting the right things done) can be a great way to get noticed for the right reasons, and helps to move your organisation forward.

Be accountable

The need to be accountable may seem obvious, but a lot of managers I've worked with over the years found ways not to be around when blame was being apportioned. This subject isn't just about blame, of course – it's also about being the person accountable for delivering on behalf of your group or function.

This ties into a lot of the other areas we've worked through – being a team player, being organised, etc., but it deserves its own (brief) section because we often forget to be accountable for our area.

In a situation where something has to be delivered, and no-one else puts up their hand, being accountable includes being willing to volunteer for things that you know you can move forward. It can be challenging to know where to draw the line between being responsible for the group's success and being a patsy, but here are a few suggestions that might help:

- If you have the skills or the resources to fix a problem, and no-one else can (or will) do it, put

up your hand. Understanding that this can have risk attached, set expectations appropriately. Becoming known as someone who can consistently deliver and is willing to go the extra mile can be career-building.
- Hold yourself accountable. Acknowledging when you are at fault, and owning the remediation of that fault is a crucial part of being responsible. Too many managers and individual contributors in my experience have played the blame game. This behaviour doesn't help anyone. Problems don't get fixed by finger-pointing. Be accountable for your mistakes.
- Be accountable for your people. If a member of your team fails in an impactful way, your job is to provide aircover, not push them under the bus. You have to enable your staff to fail safely, or they will never grow. If someone repeatedly screws up, then it's a different story – you are then accountable to manage them out of the team or organisation if they are a poor fit.
- Hold your people accountable. This is closely related to the above, but as part of the group's delivery, everyone has to know who owns the ball at a particular point in time, and what they are expected to do with it. By holding your team to account, you will demonstrate positive leadership and help your staff to grow and develop.

- Deliver, deliver, deliver. I've mentioned this above in terms of volunteering, and also in terms of being action-oriented, but delivering against your organisational goals is the reason you are collecting a paycheck. If you fail to hit the required targets, don't blame others. Again, spreading blame doesn't help. Figure out what went wrong (especially if other teams are part of the delivery chain) and make sure it doesn't happen again. Do what you say you're going to do.

Being accountable is not complicated, but like a lot of other subjects we've covered, it is hard. Being consistently accountable is very hard. It is easier to make excuses when we're tired, or we've just been subjected to a "learning moment" in front of the entire senior leadership team, or we're having difficulties at home. It is always important to act with integrity and take ownership of the things that we should.

Be a role model

A very dismissive way to put this is "Monkey see, monkey do.". In fact, in the English language, the term "aping your betters" used to be used to describe someone copying the behaviour of someone higher in the social stratum than oneself, and again, it was quite derogatory. It is imperative to understand, however, that organisations take on the behaviours and values that are exemplified by the leader or leaders of that organisation.

At one of the corporations I worked at, the head of the Network Engineering & Operations group, who were responsible for providing all Local- and Wide-Area networking technology to the company, was notoriously unhelpful. He routinely ignored requests from his peers; he failed to turn up for meetings; he didn't return phone calls. He fought tooth and nail to safeguard his budget without thinking about the bigger picture and got into screaming matches with his peers in the view of some of their staff.

His organisation was fundamental to the delivery of service for the company's clients, and he knew it – but it didn't make him any more willing to be helpful. Not coincidentally, the whole Network Engineering & Operations group had a terrible reputation – the behaviours he displayed were copied at every level in his organisation, with only the occasional break-out exception. People who didn't follow the group behaviours didn't last long. Fortunately, in the end, he was encouraged to leave, as senior managers became more and more aware of how his leadership was adversely impacting customers. Senior management appointed one of his direct reports as his successor, and the group subsequently ended up working for me as part of a broader reorganisation. During the time that I had been a customer of theirs, my view of the group had been very negative, and I expected to find that most of the barrel was rotten, if you like. What I found instead was that there were a large number of excellent technical staff in the organisation, who, with the right leadership, became collaborative and customer-focussed. My point in telling this story is to highlight just how important I have seen good leadership, and being a good role model for your team and organisation to be. Consistent bad behaviours from a leader will set the tone for the organisation, group or team for which they are responsible. Lead by example – whether you realise it or not, your staff will copy how you behave, so give them a good standard to follow, and encourage them when they exceed that standard.

Be mindful

Mindfulness may seem like a strange choice to finish this section on "Be"-ing with, but to me, this has become more and more important as I have gotten older.

Mindfulness means many things to many people. To me, it is focussing on the present moment, and acting accordingly. We often act or react on auto-pilot. We eat the cookies or doughnuts that someone has brought into the office without thinking about it, just because they're there. We don't think about our fitness or health goals at that moment – we're not mindful about what we're doing. It's incredible how much more you can eat in a food-rich environment when you're not paying attention.

When we find ourselves blindsided by an argument or verbal attack, we can emotionally react rather than rationally respond. We lose sight of any outcomes we wish to have as our amygdala-driven responses take over, and our "inner chimp" comes out to fight. Someone loaned me a copy of "The Chimp Paradox" by Steve Peters, and while I didn't connect with the writing style, I did understand the point he was trying to make – if we don't control our initial, emotionally-based response, the outcomes won't be the ones we want.

Being mindful also helps us select the right words to use to defuse a tense situation or reduce someone's stress levels. Instead of publicly criticising a staff member for failure, we remember to thank them for their efforts and then correct their behaviour constructively in private. While some people feel that public "executions" help to discourage others from making the same mistakes, I'm a firm believer that healthy organisations are safe ones, and you can't feel safe to try new things if you're afraid to make mistakes. Mindfulness, in this context, ties back firmly to the ideas in the section on "Manage your reactions".

Becoming more mindful brings a whole range of positive behaviours together. There are plenty of tools available to us to help with this. I've found mindfulness meditation to be quite helpful, but it doesn't work for everyone. I use the Headspace app, which uses guided 10- or 15-minute meditation sessions. I usually get into the office early (before 07:00), and if I find that I'm not as focussed as I would like because I haven't had a good night's sleep, or if I'm irritated because my commute didn't go well, the first thing I do is spend 10 minutes meditating.

If you're already late, does this not add to the time crunch? Yes, but it's worth it. Doing work with clarity and intent is a lot better than trying to work with a head full of irritation and frustration. And the outputs are better when your head is on straight, and you're correctly focussed. I would prefer to do less work well than more work badly – the latter usually results in more time wasted when you have to try and correct mistakes and address rework.

Like everyone, I often fail. The thing that mindfulness meditation reminds you is that failure is to be expected, whether you're counting breaths or trying to manage a challenging conversation. It is what you do next that matters – observing the failure, and then course-correcting is the response most of us would want, and the one that mindfulness teaches.

Mindfulness is a choice, and the investment in developing mindful habits is a good one, in my opinion.

Become

As we progress through our management journey, there are skills and behaviours that we can aspire to develop. Some of them are non-intuitive and take longer to build. Others are obvious, but require an intentional approach to make part of our repertoire. This section makes some suggestions as to what we could aim to become.

Become a storyteller

We've all sat through boring presentations, where someone seems intent on reading each of their million bullets on the slide verbatim, in a flat monotone. Chances are, the best presentation you've been to didn't have much in the way of presentation material – it was someone on a stage, telling you a story.

Storytelling isn't just for people trying to make a sale. It's essential for engaging audiences in a variety of formats, whether you're pitching an idea to your boss, trying to gel your team around a project or trying to secure investment.

Stories resonate with us because we've evolved to tell stories around campfires. They connect us in a way that facts-only presentations do not.

Stories have to be authentic – they have to tell personal or professional truths. They can have allegories or metaphors in them, but only as a way to move the story forward.

And they have to be relatable. If you're trying to connect with your audience, using flowery language, too much data, or experiences that most people do not share will all act as an impediment to that connection.

If you're talking about things that others will relate to and can connect to, in an authentic, honest way, you have a much better chance to engage your audience and embed the idea that you're trying to convey. And it should only be **one** idea to be successful – we're all terrible at concentrating at times, so if you bombard your audience with too many facts or concepts, the chances are they'll miss the key one. "Buy my book", "fund my project", "care because this is important", or whatever it is that you're trying to get them to focus on.

There's an excellent book on why stories are essential, titled "Storyworthy", by Matthew Dicks. He gives terrific advice on how to construct stories, and just as importantly how to recognise the stories in our own lives through "Homework for Life".

Stories aren't tricks. They are tools to help you connect with and communicate to your audience in a meaningful, lasting way. I often recommend to people I'm helping with presentations that they start with their story in mind, and build their content around the bones of the story.

Become a cheerleader

I'm not saying you have to put on a cheerleader's costume, grab some pom-poms and dance. Being a cheerleader for your team and your organisation is essential. There are an awful lot of people spreading negative messages in the world today, in your workplace and elsewhere. It's effortless to climb on that bandwagon, and agree that so-and-so sucks, or that everything is too difficult. This approach to life is classified as Stage 2 culture in Dave Logan's book "Tribal Leadership". It's a lot more challenging to consistently look for positive messages to share, and for ways to uplift your team in full view of your management structure.

To reinforce those points - don't be a spreader of negative messages, and do celebrate the successes of your people visibly. Take the failures as your own, and the achievements as your team's right. When you have a win, make sure the people who did the work get the kudos. When you've been having a challenging period, and some success is finally delivered, it is very tempting to take some of the credit personally. Don't.

If you deserve credit for leading a team to their win, you will get that credit by reflection. Your team deserve the public acclaim because, without the members of your team, nothing would get done.

Additionally, be your own cheerleader. The way we talk to ourselves in our heads can have a significant impact on our performance and overall wellbeing. Negative self-talk is not unusual (in fact, it's pretty common), but when we catch ourselves being negative towards ourselves ("I'm no good at this", "I can't do maths/science/public speaking", "I can't win", or even worse "I hate myself"), it is really important to recognise it and then work to counteract it.

By replacing negative language with positive ("I can do this!", "I've got this!", "I'm prepared, and can win!") we can reduce the negative impacts (anxiety, lack of self-esteem, failure to thrive) of negative self-talk. This approach to "reprogramming" or reframing our internal self-talk is based on the work of psychologists like Donald Meichenbaum, who helped to develop Cognitive Behavioural Modification approaches.

There is a wealth of information available on the benefits of positive self-talk, but the key is to practice and make a habit of it. Be realistic about your limits, and learn which ones are self-imposed. Recognise the self-sabotaging talk, and when you identify it, actively replace it with positive alternatives. It will make a difference in your life.

Become a critical thinker

Critical thinking is a learned skill, that many of us either fail to maintain or never had to begin with. As the father of three children, I have become intimately acquainted with the word "Why?". Usually repeated several thousand times in the day, it is how children learn. Children may not have a structured approach to learning, but they clearly understand the value of questioning things – and as they get older, they wonder about your parenting skills as well as why the world works the way it does.

For managers, critical thinking, and the ability to question intelligently is a crucial skill to develop an understanding of the challenges your team are facing and to help them understand how to overcome obstacles.

To me, critical thinking is the ability to clearly and precisely question – whether it is our motivations and actions, the proposals brought to us by members of our teams, or even the information presented to us daily through news and social media channels. It means not accepting statements at face value; questioning and thinking about what is being offered through as many angles as possible, while not getting bogged down in analysis. Asking questions like "is this source of information known to be unbiased, or is it partisan?"; "Who gains from the sharing of this information?"; "Is there an alternative interpretation of the information being presented?"; "Is this person/group/institution known to be believable?" can help to assist us in diagnosing logical or factual problems with what we're seeing or hearing. For example, a state-owned news outlet making a claim about the leader of another country should be viewed as being heavily biased in the interest of the originating state.

All of us can be led astray by our biases. Daniel Kahneman and Amos Tversky conducted multiple experiments over the years of their collaboration that demonstrated just how flawed our thinking processes are. Their work spawned a whole field of study that we now refer to as Behavioural Economics. We use shortcuts (which they called heuristics) to save mental energy. These shortcuts often produce completely inaccurate results, which we may believe in implicitly. Starting with our own thinking, and how we approach the world, is an excellent start to critically examining the information we process.

Applying critical thinking approaches with our staff also helps improve the overall outputs of our teams. Even when someone has built up a "believability weighting", to use a term that Ray Dalio refers to in "Principles", it is still important to ask clarifying questions. Training yourself and your staff to use critical thinking will make them and you better. It is often helpful to run presentations intended for a senior audience (e.g. financial proposals) through an aggressively critical audience a couple of times to check for logical errors as well as "flow".

Developing critical thinking enables us to be more confident that the decisions we're making are grounded in fact rather than belief or hearsay. Testing our logic against others, or indeed, holding two conflicting thoughts in our heads (something most of us find incredibly tricky) to examine them can be a great way to see different angles to something. Asking questions repeatedly, as in the "Five Whys" method, allows for robust analysis before critical decisions are made using often scarce resources. This "additional thinking" doesn't have to take much time. We're not looking to get into analysis paralysis here – but doing the extra mental due diligence can be vital to delivering the right long-term outcomes for a low-cost, short-term investment.

Become aware of your biases

Knowledge of personal preferences is directly linked to the previous section on Critical Thinking. We all have cognitive biases. These are not necessarily biases that lead to discrimination; for example, gender or race-related biases. The definition of cognitive bias, according to the renowned sages of Wikipedia, is:

"..a systematic pattern of deviation from a norm or rationality in judgement.~

These deviations are often described as errors – misinterpretations of data, based on faulty information processing.

A fundamental example of this kind of bias is known as Clustering, where we imply patterns from data where those patterns don't exist. In basketball, this is known as the "hot hand fallacy" – and in other areas as "being on a roll". This is the expectation that someone who is on winning streak will have a higher chance of continuing on that winning streak, whether the activity is throwing baskets, sinking putts on a golf course or correctly predicting stock market performance. The fascinating thing about "hot hand" is that division exists in the research community on how certain factors can influence human behaviour – increased confidence due to a successful shot may increase the probability of the next attempt being on target. For general pattern recognition, however, the clustering fallacy is often down to misinterpreting the data available to us. We don't do statistical analysis particularly well in real-time.

Some other cognitive errors that are particularly relevant to management are:

- The recency bias. Based on an individual's performance over the past quarter or month, they may get higher than deserved full-year performance ratings, because the reviewing manager neglects to review the full year – they can recall most easily the recent behaviours or performance of the individual, so that is what they rate.
- Anchoring bias. This bias is particularly relevant when it comes to, for example, contract or salary negotiation. The first figure or value that we hear becomes the "anchor" for the discussion, regardless of how high or low it is. Kahneman and Tversky gave some excellent examples of this in their book, and Robert Cialdini's "Influence: The Power of Persuasion" also has some significant cases.
- Confirmation bias. We often look for information that confirms a position we already hold (preconceptions, in other words). We're a lot less likely to look for information that

disproves a firmly held belief because to do so makes us uncomfortable. Social media platforms are rife with "echo chambers" where people with similar views continuously reaffirm each other.
- Sunk cost fallacy. This particular fallacy is sometimes referred to as "throwing good money after bad". If money has already been committed to a project that is failing, the money is considered to be a sunk cost – unrecoverable. Someone suffering from this fallacy tends to continue to pour money into the project, justified by the money already spent. It often takes a detached party to come in and assess the project objectively to stop the bleeding.
- Self-serving bias. People labouring under this bias often demonstrate a tendency to claim that successes are due to their talents and efforts, and failures are due to the shortcomings of others, or a lack of resources, for example. The root of this bias appears to be due to a desire to maintain self-esteem and can be toxic to organisational morale when displayed by mid- and senior-level managers.

The bias that we tend to think of most when we're discussing the workplace is discriminatory bias, which is often due to Affinity bias. This type of thinking is a set of cognitive distortions that lead us to hire and promote people who look and think like us, on the basis that they are more aligned, or "better" than other candidates. This type of bias is what we're typically trying to address with unconscious bias training for hiring managers, or other, related Diversity & Inclusion activities. In the context of hiring and promotions, requiring a diverse slate of candidates, and a diverse reviewing panel can go some way to diffusing the impact of this kind of discriminatory bias.

It is important to reiterate that everyone has cognitive biases, and our job as managers is to ensure that we're not letting what are fundamental rationality errors impact our decision-making process. We have to make sure we're deploying critical thinking practices to understand our drivers and make sure that the choices we make are in the best interest of the organisations we work for, and the people we support.

Become a culture carrier

We've talked about culture in previous sections. As you develop in your organisation, as long as you and the culture are a fit, part of your job is to promote and develop that culture. Culture can be contagious. I remember implanting bacterial or fungal cultures in an agar plate in Science classes at school, and watching as the culture grew to take over the entire substrate. In an organisation, the substrate is based on values rather than agar, and values drive principles. These in turn, if consistently applied, drive organisational and individual behaviours. Habitual behaviours are what make up a culture.

In simple equation form:

Values ➡ Principles ➡ (Consistent) Behaviours ➡ Culture

(I like the above mapping, but a senior leader who has built a global organisation of thousands of high-performing sales professionals felt that a shorter path is more accurate for his organisation. He preferred, and they live, Values=>Behaviours=Culture. The way he put it was that if the values are simple and resonate strongly enough to be adopted consistently by everyone in the organisation, that behaviours and culture will follow.)

Let's take a few examples.

If your organisational ethos is focussed on people development, or "unleashing the power of our people", as I've seen it written, make that part of how you manage your teams. Be visible in promoting learning for your staff, and live that by being a continuous learner. Encourage your team leads to free up time in the week for development activities. I once visited a site in the north of England where I was scheduled to meet with a group of junior- to mid-level managers based there. Most of them did not report to me. They were expecting that I would provide them with the latest corporate updates, and then get on with my day. Instead, I asked them several questions. One of the questions I asked was "How many of you carve out time every week for personal development?". In a group of 15 managers, not a single hand went up. My response to them was that this was not in line with the culture that we were continuously speaking about. Additionally, if they were telling their teams to spend time on learning and development, they were hypocritical.

They may not all have changed their approaches, but I'm sure the message stuck with them (because some of them told me afterwards). You can't be a cultural carrier if you don't live the culture.

Another example I've seen is organisations that talk about Diversity & Inclusion (also known as D&I, and something we'll dig into a bit more in a subsequent section). Diversity is broadly defined as having a population of staff with varied backgrounds, experiences and outlooks, and leveraging that diversity of thought to make better decisions. Inclusion is making people of all backgrounds, cultures, religions and orientations feel that they belong. I have worked in some large organisations where D&I was a regular topic of discussion at the senior management level. The reality on the ground was often very different, though. Top management teams were frequently made up of middle-aged white males, lamenting the lack of diversity. The organisation's culture was often one where people didn't feel that they belonged for several reasons:

- They didn't see anyone like them represented at senior management level.
- They didn't feel that they had a voice in the organisation as a result.
- D&I was viewed by people who most needed to feel represented as a box-ticking exercise.
- The use of non-inclusive language could be observed in the hallways, canteens and meeting rooms when people gathered.

In both of the above examples, the need for managers at all levels to live the culture the organisation espoused was utterly evident to the staff. "Do as I say, not as I do" is still the culture in a lot of companies, large and small, and creates cultural dissonance in the organisation. When that disconnect between what is said and done is evident, staff become disengaged, sometimes to the point where they will leave, but worse, often to the point where they remain but are not invested in the goals of the organisation.

As managers, all of us are responsible for improving the cultures of the organisations where we work, and for making sure that the best elements of the culture are always being displayed.

Become a D&I champion

I see being a Diversity & Inclusion (D&I) champion as being part of being a culture carrier. In too many organisations, we don't witness the society we live in being adequately represented. Within corporate America and beyond, too many senior management teams and boards are still lacking representative levels of diversity. A lack of diversity, particularly of thought, leads to what I think of as "middle-aged white male syndrome." People who have all gone to the same schools or colleges, belong to the same professional organisations, have progressed through the same career paths, and consequently, all have similar blind-spots. There is a significant body of research done by HBR and other organisations that shows the value of diverse management teams.

Diversity isn't just desirable or the right thing to do from a societal perspective. It has real financial benefits for organisations that choose to prioritise it. McKinsey have published research that shows that companies that are in the top quartile for gender and ethnic diversity are more likely to have financial returns above national industry medians. A study published by Boston Consulting Group in 2018 showed that diverse leadership teams boost innovation; and a 19% increase in innovation-related revenue above companies with lower diversity.

Many of the tech firms focus heavily on increasing the diversity of their management structures. Google has taken an approach that Ray Dalio would term radical transparency, and publish an annual diversity report showing how they have done against their targets for hiring and retention. In both tech firms and the financial services industry, there is a significant focus on increasing the diversity of teams and boards, to develop more diverse thinking.

From an inclusion perspective, the focus on helping people belong is critical. Creating a diverse organisation only works if the different individuals you bring together can coalesce around a single set of values and outcomes. Inclusion means that people have to feel comfortable that the work they are doing aligns to their values, and also that the cultural messages align to organisational behaviour.

Becoming a D&I champion may be an additional formal role in your organisation, or it may just be the way that you choose to behave. For companies with more substantial structures, formal D&I programs are often in place, can be funded, and have tracked results. Getting involved in a structured program can be a great way of helping to drive organisational change, and can also be a way to increase your awareness of the organisation to which you belong. A bonus is that D&I work is often seen as being a good indicator of someone's ability to focus on more significant issues, and can, therefore, be a precursor to a broader role.

If your organisation doesn't have a focus on Diversity & Inclusion, it definitely should. Creating a grass-roots structure to help build that cultural element can only be a good thing. The more people feel valued for who they are, the more likely they are to become fully engaged with the company and its goals. Highly engaged employees are to be found throughout the world's most successful companies. Disengaged employees, on the other hand, are consuming company resources for less than the optimal return.

Become a mentor

Why would anyone at an early stage in his or her career want to become a mentor? Let me put the question to you another way. How many times have you wished that someone had pointed out a problematic behaviour or a better approach to doing something early on in your career before you had to learn painful lessons yourself? As I noted in the introduction, painful lessons stick, but a mentor can help you identify those lessons by observation rather than experience.

By becoming a mentor, in addition to helping more junior staff members develop, you will also develop and learn yourself. In surgical teaching, there has been a traditional approach to learning how to do medical procedures – See One, Do One, Teach One. While this has been called into question as a teaching method in recent years due to concerns about patient safety, there is a lot of value in the concept of cementing knowledge by teaching.

For example, if you want to learn to perform a new procedure (whatever that might be), first you have to learn about what that procedure is. By then running through an instance of it, often guided by a teacher or by documentation, you start the first steps of embedding it in your brain. Finally, by teaching someone else, you are forced to fully comprehend all of the steps in the procedure to be able to convey it accurately to someone else.

By mentoring, whether individuals or groups, we are forced to prepare for sessions by reading up on relevant topics, refreshing our understanding of the subjects in question, and often have "aha!" moments when discussing those topics with our mentees.

I have had the privilege of mentoring both individuals and groups. While I enjoy meeting people one-to-one and understanding what I can do to help them develop, at this point, I almost prefer to mentor groups. The reason for this preference is that more often than not, I can see the members of the group teach each other. Having diverse groups of mentees seems to work best – people from different cultural backgrounds, at various stages of their careers and of mixed genders will have had different experiences. After making the environment safe for people to talk freely (some initial ground rules help, and honesty from the "senior mentor" about challenges they have faced themselves can be useful to establish safety), mentees are often willing to talk about things that are very personal in the hope of either getting help or helping one another.

Here are a few recommendations for establishing a mentoring arrangement.

- Identify whether existing mentoring programs exist in your organisation – your HR department is usually a good starting point. If there is an established program, volunteer through that to be a mentor.
- If no such program exists, suggest to your HR department that it might be useful to build one – whether it is labelled a mentoring program or something like a buddy system.
- When interacting with junior staff who are looking for help, make it known that you are willing to be a mentor if they think that would be helpful. Again, you don't have to use the words "mentor" and "mentee" to help guide someone.
- In your first session with a mentee or group, establish ground rules and expectations.
    - Find out why the individuals feel that a mentoring relationship will be helpful to them
    - Identify what it is they are trying to achieve, and how you can help with that.

- Make it clear what their responsibilities are. For example, if you recommend that they read a book or section from a book, or conduct some networking activities in between your sessions, the expectation is that they will do that. They are responsible for scheduling mentoring sessions and for ensuring they take place.
- Make it clear what your responsibilities are as a mentor. You are not there to find them a new job, for example. You are there to help them with agreed areas of development, and maybe to act as an advocate and provide introductions.
- Agree on logistics – how often the sessions will take place, how many will take place, and what success will look like (i.e. what are the desired outcomes).
- Agree how the mentoring relationship will end, either by mutual agreement or by a particular number of sessions. Mentoring engagements are all about relationships – if the mentor and mentee don't "click", it is a good thing to recognise that and walk away with no hard feelings.

Mentoring can be challenging, but in my experience, it is highly rewarding. It is a great opportunity both to learn and to give back to your organisation. And it can be very satisfying to see someone you mentored progressing in the organisation – even more so when they exceed their expectations of themselves.

Become a volunteer

I have heard and read apocryphally that the stated position for enlisted men in many armies has traditionally been "Never volunteer for anything". That may be understandable if the context is that volunteering means you're in the first wave going "over the top" in World War I trench warfare, for example.

The kind of volunteering I'm talking about is less likely to result in immediate death; in fact, it may prolong your life and improve your health. This Harvard Business review article for example, quotes a Carnegie Mellon study that shows a benefit between volunteering and mental and physical health. According to the study, people who volunteered regularly had lower blood pressure and stress levels, both of which are contributory factors to improved health outcomes.

If you've ever volunteered to help in your community, at a local school, for example, or a "Science Technology Engineering Maths" (STEM) event, you'll know that there is a shared sense of purpose among those volunteering. The general feeling is a positive one and, having completed the day or event, people leave feeling that they have done something worthwhile. I've been fortunate enough to be a speaker at STEM events, and have built bicycles for charities as part of a leadership event, but there are many ways to volunteer. You could spend time teaching adults to read, or volunteer to clean up a local beach, or share your skills with a charitable organisation.

These events don't just benefit the target community. They are also worthwhile for the participants, and for more reasons than I have cited above. Volunteering can be a great way to build a diverse network of like-minded individuals. The chances are that the people you meet at a volunteering event will carry elements of that shared sense of purpose beyond just that particular event.

Meeting like-minded people can be very reaffirming, and can lead to opportunities for further volunteering and also for career development.

If you work in a large building or campus, it can be beneficial to become a first aid volunteer. The training you receive may help you save the life of a colleague, and is transferrable outside of the work environment. Being trained in the use of CPR, and defibrillators, for example, can be a lifesaver in many contexts. It might even help you save the life of a family member.

There is also the volunteering that you can do at the local level within your team or broader organisation. I make a habit of asking colleagues at the end of each conversation if there is anything I can do to help them. More often than not, the answer is "no", but by offering to assist, I demonstrate that I am concerned about their success. When they do have something they want my help with, it often allows me to meet new people or learn something new, both of which are generally beneficial.

There are many possible ways of volunteering, but the critical thing is that to do so takes us outside of ourselves and removes our focus on our own needs, wants and desires. This external focus helps both in gaining perspective (nothing puts your life challenges into perspective like volunteering at a children's hospice, for example) and in building connections with a broader community of people.

By volunteering, we do good for others and ourselves.

Become a (good) leader

Leadership and management have many areas of overlap, and there are many definitions for both. There is a quote attributed to Peter Drucker which says "Management is doing things right. Leadership is doing the right things." This statement to me sounds like a definition of verification versus validation ("Did we do the what we said we were going to do?" as opposed to "Is what we said we were going to do the right thing?"). With the utmost respect to Peter Drucker, who knew more and wrote more on the two subjects than I ever will (The Effective Executive is the precursor to so many other books on management), I don't think his quote fully helps us define what makes a leader versus a manager.

There's a Steve Jobs quote which draws a distinct line between the two disciplines (and they are disciplines if done correctly) – "Management is about persuading people to do things they do not want to do, while leadership is about inspiring people to do things they never thought they could."

In this context, I prefer the second quote. Good leadership (and after all, we want to be good leaders) should be clear, inspiring, motivating. It can be challenging to define what constitutes good leadership, and history has many examples of "bad" leaders who were highly effective. General Stanley McChrystal has some interesting comparisons of historical leaders in his book "Leaders: Myth and Reality", where he compares leadership styles that are as diverse as those represented by Albert Einstein, Coco Chanel and Abu Musab Al Zarqawi.

Some of the people he reviewed were "bad" leaders in the current context, but are famous for their leadership because they built lasting brands, or led ideological movements, whatever we might think of their goals.

To me, leadership has many aspects of management embedded in it – communications, curiosity, positivity, for example. Being positive, confident and optimistic are fundamental traits of successful leaders because they have to carry entire organisations with them when they lead. Being positive doesn't mean being unrealistic – but it does mean not allowing your challenges to come into work with you, or your worries for the business to transmit themselves to the organisation you're responsible for. People look to leaders to determine how they should behave. If the leader is hangdog and downbeat, the organisation they lead will follow suit. (Note thatthe same is true of managers.)

There's a sort of passive-aggressive phrase I've heard from both senior and junior people in response to the "How are you?" question we often ask when starting a conversation. It is "I'm just peachy". An alternative, but equally awful term is "Living the dream". Both imply that the complete opposite is the case. The person using the phrase is essentially saying "everything sucks, but I'm pseudo-pretending that it doesn't". Hearing this type of response from a leader always concerns me, because it indicates an inherently negative mindset, which can be contagious in the organisations that they lead.

I've heard varying arguments during my career that good leaders are charismatic. I think this is pretty unhelpful because "charisma" isn't something you can develop like a muscle. If someone assumes a "charismatic mask" that is out of alignment with their true nature, the inauthenticity will become evident in both direct and subtle ways. We like authenticity in a leader because it helps to foster trust. Subtle signals that someone may not be who they claim to be can be very damaging to trust, so when it comes to charisma, my feeling is that it is less important than it used to be considered to be. On this topic, don't "fake it 'til you make it".

We often think of leaders as being at the head of an organisation. It's important to note that it is possible to lead from all levels within a company or organisational structure. Identifying gaps in leadership and then stepping in to fill them can help you advance in your career – however, don't be too quick to jump in. Understand the context in which the leadership gap has appeared, have an idea of what the correct steps are to address the issue and then take action.

Highly functional organisations not only encourage leadership at all levels; they also create circumstances that allow individuals to step forward safely to explore those opportunities.

Conclusion

The management journey is one that is continuously challenging, fraught with peril and never-ending. It is also highly rewarding from a developmental and relationship-building viewpoint. During my working life, I have moved from being primarily focussed on managing technology to being far more interested in managing and leading people. I'm not alone in this, but I'm also aware that a management career path does not suit everyone. We have to be intentional about why we are embarking on a management career, and be explicit with ourselves and others about where our development opportunities are.

Management and leadership are all about accomplishing (hopefully great) things through others. As disciplines, they are centred on helping the people we work with to develop into the best versions of themselves. They are about addressing inequities in our organisations; creating opportunities; encouraging and cheerleading, and taking total ownership for the circumstances and outcomes we have signed up to deliver.

We achieve these things by being intellectually curious; being emotionally intelligent, kind, honest and authentic; by pushing when we need to and holding back when required. We build organisations that are successful by blending thought and consideration with an appetite for action and forward momentum. In their book "The Dichotomy of Leadership", Jocko Willink and Leif Babin make it clear that accomplishing these things requires an understanding of the multiple sides to every situation. They are brutally honest about how difficult it can be to deal with the dichotomies presented by these disciplines, but they are also clear that by taking ownership of those things that we are responsible for, it is is possible to be highly successful.

What does success look like in management and leadership? Organisations that are better when we leave them than when we took on responsibility for them. Individuals who shine because of the environments we create. Customers who are consistently scoring near the top of the scale for satisfaction with the products and services our companies or organisations provide them. Diverse and inclusive working environments that reflect our societies and behave in ethical and equitable ways. Cultures that make people proud to come to work and to announce their affiliation with the organisation.

These are big marks to hit. I am hoping that in some way, the advice that I have provided in the proceeding pages will help you in making your mark in creating positive, highly functional workplaces.

Thank you for taking the time to make this journey with me, and for your support in purchasing a copy of the book.

I wish you well in your management adventure and hope that you will share what you learn with your peers. I would also be happy to hear from you at herdingcats@amusingmulcahy.com.

Best of luck!

Acknowledgements

During many Oscar Awards speeches people tend to thank their parents. I genuinely want to thank my mother - if it weren't for her, I obviously wouldn't be here - but it's more than that. She made me who I am. Her view of people and their importance has stayed with me. During her working life as a nurse she cared for people and demonstrated the value in treating everyone with dignity and respect.

I would also like to thank my proof-readers:

- Jim Mulcahy
- John Mulcahy
- Katrina Mulcahy (Comerford)
- Lia Mulcahy
- Richard Dickens
- Orla Ryan
- Suzanne Janse Van Rensburg

Without their input this book would have been a poorer effort.

Bibliography

This is just a short list of some of the writing that informed this book. For more recommendations visit https://www.amusingmulcahy.com/what-im-reading

Anything You Want - Derek Sivers

Discipline Equals Freedom: Field Manual – Jocko Willink

Extreme Ownership – Jocko Willink, Leif Babin

Grit - Angela Duckworth

How to Manage – Jo Owen

How to Lead - Jo Owen

Make Your Bed - William McRaven

The Culture Code – David Coyle, et. al.

The Five Dysfunctions of a Team - Patrick Lencioni

The Leadership Pipeline – Ram Charan, et. al.

Thinking, Fast and Slow – Daniel Kahneman

Turn The Ship Around! - David Marquet

Principles: Life and Work - Ray Dalio

Links Reference

P33 - wrote a post - https://www.amusingmulcahy.com/metrics-madness/

P58 - shown to improve mental focus - https://www.psychologytoday.com/us/blog/you-illuminated/201204/brain-scans-show-how-meditation-improves-mental-focus

P58 - believed to be decreasing - https://learningsolutionsmag.com/articles/1440/brain-science-focuscan-you-pay-attention

P94 - PubMed article - https://www.ncbi.nlm.nih.gov/pubmed/20920513

P115 - company blog post - https://www.zappos.com/about/stories/customer-service-things-to-know

P124 - Ted talks - https://www.ted.com/talks/angela_lee_duckworth_grit_the_power_of_passion_and_perseverance?language=en

P152 - McKinsey have published research - https://www.mckinsey.com/business-functions/organization/our-insights/why-diversity-matters

P153 - annual diversity report - https://diversity.google/annual-report/

P158 - This Harvard Business review article - https://www.health.harvard.edu/blog/volunteering-may-be-good-for-body-and-mind-201306266428

Printed in Great Britain
by Amazon